# TEACHER TALK

# TEACHER TALK

## Multicultural Lesson Plans
## for the Elementary Classroom

### Deborah B. Eldridge
*United States International University*

Allyn and Bacon
Boston   London   Toronto   Sydney   Tokyo   Singapore

Library of Congress Cataloging-in-Publication Data

```
Eldridge, Deborah B.
    Teacher talk : multicultural lesson plans for the elementary
  classroom / Deborah B. Eldridge.
      p.   cm.
    Includes bibliographical references (p.  ).
    ISBN 0-205-26762-9
    1. Multicultural education--United States.  2. Education,
  Elementary--United States.   I. Title.
  LC1099.3.E45  1997
  370.117'0973--dc21                                    97-19607
                                                        CIP
```

Printed in the United States of America

10 9 8 7 6 5 4 3 2    01 00 99 98

# Contents

## CHAPTER ONE

## CHAPTER TWO

# CHAPTER THREE

# CHAPTER FOUR

## CHAPTER FIVE

**How's the weather? Incorporating a multicultural approach toward meteorology** ................................................................. 91
by Tina Waters

# CHAPTER SIX

# CHAPTER SEVEN

**Maya and Aztec:  A study of the ancient Mexican civilizations .**    152
by Karen Kellogg

## CHAPTER EIGHT

**Multicultural literary guide: A teacher's companion to independent reading in the early elementary grades** ....................................  **181**
by Doug West

## ASSESSMENT APPENDIX

## REFERENCE APPENDIX

# Preface

There is a quote attributed to Kurt Vonnegut, Jr. which I often share with teachers in introductory courses in multicultural education. Somehow it seems to articulate what elementary teachers sometimes believe about what they teach. There is this lingering hope that in what we do, as teachers, we can spare the children our mistakes. But Vonnegut said it better:

> I've often thought there ought to be a manual to hand to little kids, telling them what kind of planet they're on, why they don't fall off it, how much time they've probably got here, how to avoid poison ivy and so on. I tried to write one once. It was called 'Welcome to Earth'. But I got stuck explaining why we don't fall off the planet. Gravity is just a word. It doesn't explain anything. If I could get past gravity, I'd tell them how we reproduce, how long we've been here, apparently, a little bit about evolution. And one thing I would really like to tell them about is cultural relativity. I didn't learn until I was in college about all the other cultures, and I should have learned that in first grade. A first grader should understand that his or her culture isn't a rational invention; that there are thousands of other cultures and they all work pretty well; that all cultures function on faith rather than truth; that there are lots of alternatives to our own society. Cultural relativity is defensible and attractive. It's also a source of hope. It means we don't have to continue this way if we don't like it.

This book is written for teachers, who understand what Vonnegut was saying and who, rightly, wonder if they are doing the right thing in the right way at the right time.

I, for one, think there are many right things, and right ways, and right times. And this book is an attempt to show you what I mean. I strongly believe that teachers should be celebrated for what they are able to accomplish and appreciated for the complexities that their school settings and populations bring to the instructional choices that they have to make. Each of the seven chapters which follow is written by a real, working classroom teacher who is struggling with the issues of multicultural education across a variety of levels, content areas, and personal interests. The teachers tell their stories, present their curriculum units, discuss their concerns, and describe themselves. This is a book founded in the real world of everyday practice and brings out the voices of those who are held accountable on a daily basis for what they teach, or choose not to teach.

In a completely teacher-designed, classroom-tested, user-friendly format, the seven teachers in this book present their unique responses to the questions "What can I do to integrate multicultural education into my classroom?" and "How do I begin to do it?" Grounded in the theories of well-known multicultural educators such as James Banks, Christine Sleeter, and Carl Grant, the teachers' instructional units for elementary classrooms include practically everything other educators would need in order to implement the units. Adaptations are encouraged. The units can be used as a catalyst for creating other, even more unique responses to the challenges of multiculturalism. Each unit contains lesson plans which include objectives, time periods for implementation, materials, procedures, and homework or assessment suggestions. Additionally, the teachers who designed and field-tested these units share their rationales for the lessons, their concerns during implementation, and the uniqueness of the educational settings which motivated their responses.

The book also gives college and university educators an opportunity to learn what teachers are doing in their classrooms. Here is a book which illustrates the "how" of multicultural education by teachers who understand the "why". The authors encourage the use of their examples as a basis for discussion, debate, and articulation of the complexities of bringing theory into practice. Above all this book is an opportunity for teachers themselves to be heard as they struggle with the art of teaching for a changing and increasingly multicultural world.

In the foreword to Pedagogy of the Oppressed by Paulo Friere, Richard Shaull makes the following point:

> There is no such thing as a neutral educational process.
> Education either functions as an instrument which is used
> to facilitate the integration of the younger generation

into the logic of the present system and bring about conformity to it, or it becomes 'the practice of freedom,' the means by which men and women deal critically and creatively with reality and discover how to participate in the transformation of their world.

For the teachers who read this book, and for the children who benefit from their reading of it, may you discover how to participate in transforming our world for the better.

# Acknowledgements

In addition to the seven teacher/contributors, there are three people and one company that deserve to be acknowledged for the parts they contributed to the completion of this book. Without them its pages would be drab, dreary, and not at all representative of the joy we experienced in creating it. Expert Software, Inc. gave permission to use many of the images from their software "3500 Color Clip Art Images" and "3500 Color Clip Art #2" on CD-Rom. Chapter title graphics and many of the student handouts, homework letters, activity sheets, and assessment measures contain an image from those two collections. These images are Copyrighted © 1994-97 by Expert Software, Inc., Media Graphics International, Inc., and Imageline Graphics, Inc.

Sean Van Tyne and Kari Martin are two individuals whose creativity and artistic skills enriched the rest of the pages in the book. Handouts, activity sheets, parent letters, and instructions have been enlivened by their original drawings. I thank them, and I admire them for the ease with which they can bring a raw idea to life in a way that engages children.

One more acknowledgement is owed to a retired librarian, Harriet Venable, who told me that her knowledge might be "obsolete" when I turned to her for much needed advice. "Obsolescence" is something I think is wired into machinery, not human beings. Without Mrs. Venable's timely and tireless research and suggestions, there would be two lessons sorely in need of a lyric, or two.

# Dedication

I dedicate this book to the memory of my father.

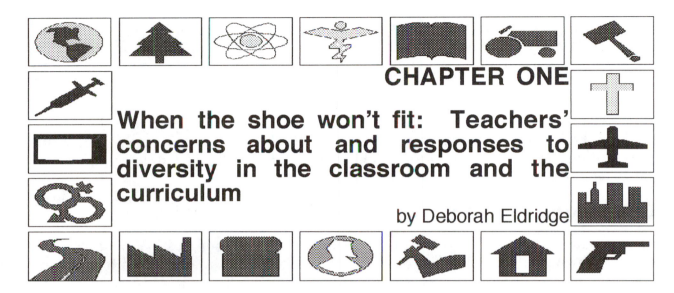

# CHAPTER ONE

## When the shoe won't fit: Teachers' concerns about and responses to diversity in the classroom and the curriculum

by Deborah Eldridge

Shoebox.

I'd meant to say soapbox but it came out shoebox. And there I was caught flatfooted saying I'd take this opportunity to get up on my shoebox. The roomful of teachers to whom I was presenting an in-service workshop on multicultural education laughed with me.

Perhaps, however, I'd meant it that way. Perhaps the shoebox was a metaphor for many of the conclusions of much of the research I'd read on culture, literacy, and the child. Time and time again I'd moan as a perfectly elegant, distinctive, and important piece of work reduced itself to the most commonplace, ordinary, simplistic suggestions for implementation. Shoebox solutions.

In the not so distant past, for example, the individual classroom teacher bore the load for diversity in classroom instruction. Repeatedly, culture and literacy related studies called for a more negotiating-type dialogue between classroom teachers and their students (Arreaga-Mayer & Greenwood, 1986; Bissex, 1988; Cazden, 1983, 1985; Cochran-Smith, 1984; Fillion, 1988; Heath, 1983.1986; Taylor, 1988; Tharp & Gallimore, 1989; Wells, 1985; among others). Not that it was a bad suggestion.

While well-meaning, such suggestions were laden with hidden messages that were less than so. To suggest adopting a more "negotiating" style with students places the entire burden of responding to students' cultural differences squarely on the shoulders of the individual teacher. No mention is made of the complications of a behavioral, one-way model of curriculum, Eurocentric instructional materials, or teacher in-service training and professional development which is often less focused on teacher needs than on administrative "priorities." Nor is mention made of administrative or societal responsibilities for the current inequities, nor the power school cultures wield to support or block significant reform, even if a teacher were to attempt modifications within the confines of his/her individual classroom.

The point is that the situation in schools and classrooms regarding instruction and cultural diversity is far too complex to suggest that the adoption of a negotiating style on the part of the teacher will improve performance for children whose culture differs from that of the majority of students. It's not that simple.  A shoebox just won't hold it all.

And teachers know it.  And yet are torn by their continued sense of individual responsibility for the students--their "children".  And they ask hard, tough questions about what they can do and how they can do it.

## Challenges for the classroom and the curriculum

In the context of Masters' courses in multicultural education, I have worked with teachers throughout Southern California.  They come to the classes with concerns. Concerns that are based in experience.  They bring experience in classrooms where as many as nineteen different languages are spoken, and where the teacher's culture may be shared by a minority of the students.  In other classrooms, where the drama of diversity is minimal, the students are encased within a glass cage of economic segregation, which is at odds with out-of-school experiences, life in Southern California, and wider world context.  These teachers don't need to be convinced that accommodating diversity in their instruction is a necessity.  They know it, see it, and feel it every day. But they have concerns.  Legitimate ones.

Some of the primary questions that teachers ask are:  How do I incorporate a respect for diversity into the curriculum?  How much more will I have to teach in a limited time?  How do I address all this stuff without losing my strength in academics? How can I fit this in with all the other curricula?

Contained within these questions are two underlying misconceptions that need to be addressed. One misconception is that diversity issues and multicultural concerns must be handled separately from what a teacher is already doing in the classroom. The other misconception is that addressing diversity and multiculturalism will result in the "watering down" of the curriculum.  Not so in both cases.

Incorporating diversity into the classroom and curriculum does not mean that a teacher has to take away from what is already occurring.  The very best culturally sensitive teaching that I have seen was the result of "focusing" on the curriculum in a new way, not adding to it.

Grant and Sleeter (1989) and Sleeter and Grant (1993) have taken a thorough look at what this kind of "refocus" of the curriculum entails by identifying five approaches to multicultural education.  In my work with Masters' teachers, we examine each of these five approaches to multicultural education and select some component of the classroom curriculum to refocus in similar ways.   I ask the teachers not to create something totally new, but to put a multicultural "spin" on something they are already doing in their classrooms.

The first approach identified by Sleeter and Grant is classified as "Teaching the Culturally Different." These classroom practices stem from a belief that the business of the classroom is to prepare the culturally different student for participation in the mainstream society. From this perspective students' cultures are accommodated by building bridges between them and the school's demands.

Joan, for example, is a second grade teacher in a fairly diverse, small town elementary school. Her classroom approach is very person-centered and holistic in its treatment of the core subject areas of reading, writing, and mathematics. Joan felt that she wanted to create a connection between the cultural differences of her students and the reading and writing experiences she was providing in her classroom. From her goals a language arts unit emerged in which students link their homes to the classroom through shared activities on the diversity of family history within the context of multicultural literature (see Chapter 2). Joan remarked, "I attempted to draw from the personal experiences of the children and their families." However, the connections continue, as Joan noted, because "through these personal experiences they begin to build bridges between themselves and children of different ethnicities and cultures" as well. Joan's classroom would have offered reading and writing experiences to her students much like the unit she designed. Her goals did not change. However, she brought the students' home cultures into the classroom and linked them to instruction by simply researching some variations in the literature and constructing themes through which she addressed her goals.

A second approach to curricular refocus is referred to by Sleeter and Grant as the "Human Relations Approach." By far the most common of the five approaches, these classroom practices emerge from a commitment to tolerance, students' self-esteem, and the reduction of stereotypes. Students' cultures and contributions are appreciated through cooperative activities, classroom decorations, and lessons about similarities and differences.

Kelly, an elementary teacher in a linguistically and ethnically diverse community west of Los Angeles, chose to focus a series of lessons on providing alternatives to traditional holiday activities. Bothered by the exclusivity of "Ghosts and Goblins" for Halloween and "Santa Claus" for Christmas, Kelly attempted to maintain some of the special excitement classes experience during these times by offering her students opportunities to explore cultures, artifacts, and folk art practices (see Chapter 3). "The project was well-received by the parents," she noted after her mask unit. "Of the parents who were normally quite concerned about Halloween, not one objected to this project. They appreciated the multicultural and artistic value of the unit, a shift from the traditional Halloween festivities in which they saw little educational merit."

Another approach to multicultural education is referred to as the "Single Group Studies Approach." In this approach a particular group or culture is singled out for in-depth study and appreciation from the perspective of that culture. These classroom practices acknowledge social inequalities, strive to raise students' consciousness, and promote social activism.

Karen, a sixth grade teacher in a racially mixed middle school, focused her instructional adaptation on a Single Group Studies approach to the standard curriculum unit on "ancient" cultures.  With Mexico a brief two-hour drive to the south and a school population of predominantly Mexican-American students, Karen designed a unit of study to include the ancient Mexican civilizations (see Chapter 7).  "At least this allows more of my students to see some of their own heritage in what we study," she commented.   "And it allows the other students to know that Mexico's contributions to world civilization were not minimal as might be inferred from the Greco-Roman and Egyptian focus of traditional 'ancient' culture studies."

The fourth and fifth approaches are called the "multicultural education" and "multicultural and social reconstructionist" approaches.  The two approaches share the common goals of promoting social equality and cultural pluralism.  However, the social reconstructionist approach puts greater emphasis on the active participation of students in righting the wrongs in society.

Barbara, a sixth grade teacher in an upper middle class neighborhood school, adapted her state-mandated lessons on the three primary documents of the United States (Bill of Rights, Declaration of Independence, and Constitution).  Previously, she had focused the lessons from a text-based, Eurocentric perspective which told the tale of these documents devoid of the conflicts and exclusions of women and people of color. Her "refocus" invigorated the unit by examining these documents from multiple perspectives (see Chapter 6). As Barbara rethought her lessons, she integrated math, writing, and reading into the standard Social Studies unit.  And, though it was a lot of work, "I loved doing this," she said. "I like history and it was fun to search out new information.  There's so much they don't tell us about the history of our country and there's so little available for children.  I feel like I've done something really important here."  And she had.

Though initially perplexed by the suggestion that infusing multicultural approaches throughout the curriculum can be accomplished without adding on or diminishing anything, each of these teachers was able to adopt a theoretical perspective which allowed them to shift their classroom focus toward more culturally sensitive practices.  None of these teachers was willing to sacrifice the strength of their academic program to  diversity.  And they didn't.  In contrast, all felt that their programs were strengthened by what they had done.  Nor had they "added on" an additional thirty-minute lesson to accommodate issues of diversity.  They had begun to understand that addressing diversity means rethinking what they were already doing and, in many ways, making it better. What felt, initially, like a burden gave way to an exciting exploration of possibilities within their own classrooms. They had fun.

However,  not all of the teachers' concerns about issues of diversity and multicultural education were so specifically classified as  "how to" create a match between diversity and existing curriculum. Instead, some of their questions focused on creating curriculum that addresses diversity as an issue in and of itself. What should be taught about diversity and how much? How do I teach acceptance of different cultures? How do I help kids with differences? How can kids be more accepting of diversity?

A standard response to these types of teacher questions has been to point them toward the multicultural children's literature. Share books, lots of books, get to know the multicultural literature that's out there, use it, read it, write about it. This suggestion implies that the "best" way to teach diversity is to model it through literature. Certainly there is consensus that:

> Literature plays a strong role in helping us understand and value our cultural heritage as well. Developing positive attitudes toward our own culture and the cultures of others is necessary for both social and personal development. Carefully selected literature can illustrate the contributions and values of the many cultures. It is especially critical to foster an appreciation of the heritage of the ethnic minorities in American society.... Literature can contribute considerably toward our understanding and thus our respect (Norton, 1991, p. 2).

Doug, an ex-military officer making a career switch into education, adopted a multicultural approach to confronting issues of diversity by compiling a guide to multicultural literature. He rightly believed that purchasing a few of the popular titles was not sufficient for any classroom. What a new teacher, like himself, needed to do was to establish a set of criteria by which to judge existing materials and to evaluate the appropriateness of new ones (see Chapter 8). Doug readily admits that "I initially struggled to find books." However, as he began to read and refine his guidelines, he was better able to identify books which exposed children to "authentic, culturally conscious literature."

Other suggestions for "teaching" diversity include utilizing specialized curriculum kits and packages which address diversity as a separate subject ("World of Difference," and other human relations curriculum programs). Such kits include lessons about accepting each others' differences and seeking the similarities in all of us. This suggestion implies that lessons in diversity cannot be inferred, but need to be focused upon specifically in order to be generalized.

However, there is some evidence to suggest that isolating instruction may, in fact, compartmentalize its effect. Research on the features necessary for any training procedure to be generalized (Brown & Campione, 1981) suggests that an important component is to train in multiple settings to alleviate the problem of "welding." Thus, instructional units or lessons which focus on diversity training need to be integrated throughout the curriculum and not performed in isolation from daily, ongoing practices.

Another approach to "teaching" diversity is to focus on the potential for conflict and, therefore, to teach resolution skills, cooperative group strategies, and peer counseling techniques.  This approach implies that the central issue in diversity is divisiveness and instructional settings should address the skills to deal with conflict.  These are not necessarily bad suggestions.  In fact, they are very important ideas to keep in mind.

However, there are perspectives on these concerns which need to be articulated.  If we continue the metaphor of shoebox solutions, then the instructional options of multicultural literature, teaching similarities and differences, and focusing on conflict resolution are clearly not enough in and of themselves.  On the one hand, the idea of teaching tolerance or acceptance of diversity is quite popular in some circles.  On the other hand, as Carlos Cortes (1995) pointed out in his "Distinguished Lecture on Critical Issues" at the National Conference of the Association for Supervision and Curriculum Development,  "imagine after 10 years of marriage that your partner comes to you and says that s/he has learned to tolerate you."  It's a point well taken.  How pleased would any of us be with a statement of this kind?  If there is teaching to be done which is strictly focused on issues of diversity, then let's target a more complimentary outcome.  Or a more essential one.

Banks (1995) suggests that reducing prejudice is one of five dimensions of any program in multicultural education.  Reviewing the literature, he notes that there are some indications that a democratic curriculum (Trager & Yarrow, 1952), an intercultural curriculum (Hayes & Conklin, 1953), and/or curricular  materials and interventions (Fisher, 1965; Leslie & Leslie, 1972; Yawkey, 1973; Lessing & Clarke, 1976; Litcher & Johnson, 1969; Litcher, Johnson & Ryan, 1973; and Shirley, 1988)  can modify racial attitudes.

A combined curricular materials and intervention approach was adopted by Mickey, an elementary teacher in a gifted, combination first and second grade classroom setting.  Disturbed by the lack of cultural appreciation in their school, a group of parents had pushed for some changes.  The school agreed to study the cultures of their community in depth over  a number of weeks.  Mickey's colleagues selected Japan as a focus, and Mickey went to work finding all that she could about the people and culture to share with her inquisitive students.   "My goal was to include art, music, the flag, geography, population, celebrations, homes, food, language, numbers, clothing, and history."   Mickey pointed out,   "Through studying similarities and differences of our two cultures, I hoped my students would gain respect, tolerance, and understanding for another group of people."  Her unit (see Chapter 4) serves as a model of the kind of curricular materials and interventions that can be created for very young children by a teacher committed  to reducing prejudice.

Tina, a fourth grade teacher in a homogeneous  suburban setting, adopted another approach by creating an intercultural unit for the science curriculum.    Believing that her students needed knowledge and experience of cultural and economic diversity, Tina created a meteorology unit in which she linked ethnic studies and global education (see Chapter 5). "I think they really enjoyed the freedom that tends to result from studying issues from many viewpoints,"  she remarked.  "Students began to feel confident that their ideas weren't necessarily wrong just because they weren't 'in the book,' or straight from my mouth.  It is also a great relief when students realize that more than one answer is acceptable if it can be justified." Prejudice reduction can be initiated through intercultural curriculum which extends beyond language arts into the diversity and acceptability of perspectives in such areas as science and mathematics.

Each of these teachers adopted a response to "teaching diversity" which targeted prejudice reduction by integrating their approaches into what they were already doing. They didn't want to separate out and pinpoint any one group or skill.  On the contrary, they maintained their focus on quality education and embedded significant student outcomes and curricular reforms within the context of the everyday activities of the living and learning communities of their classrooms.

## Meeting the challenges alone and together

Even tougher questions are posed by the teachers who ask,  How do you teach the children when the "attitude" comes from home?  How do we convince our community of the need for multicultural education?  We teach it in the classroom but if it vanishes with the outside wind, what can we do?  Good points.  Are teachers fighting a losing battle?  Swimming upstream?  Offering to spoon a mountain of prejudice into a shoebox?

Maybe so.  Maybe the shoebox was a metaphor for what the field of education does with significant questions, vital issues, and advances in understanding.  Too often large issues are transformed into cute kits:  colorful cards and reproducibles for a teacher's quick reference and easy use.  I can picture a slick shoebox promising "250 Ways to a Cultural Classroom"  and offering neatly catalogued reference cards with "easy-vue" dividers:  parent activities, community events, listening skills, reading, writing, games, bulletin boards, holidays, and celebrations.  Oh, dear.

The teachers are absolutely correct in the issues they raise.  There is something missing in all of this.  Something elusive.  Something significant.  Something promising.  Something that gets at these tougher, deeper concerns.

Some time ago, when attempting to broaden the focus of intervention on behalf of minority students, Cummins (1986) wrote about "empowering."  Though a concept that has become something of a cliché, empowerment might be a useful way to conceptualize teacher involvement in multicultural education as something other than a one-way process with the teacher at the dispensing end and the student in "receivership."   However, empowerment needs to include something bigger than the classroom.

Cummins argued convincingly that "four structural elements in the organization of schooling contribute to the extent to which minority students are empowered or disabled" (p. 24).  These elements are:  the extent to which students' language and culture are incorporated into the school program, the extent to which communities are empowered through interaction with the school, the extent to which students collaborate with the teacher in learning and sharing control, and the extent to which assessment professionals become advocates for minority students.   In Cummins' framework, the importance and value of teachers and classrooms are upheld but the burden of responsibility for reform is placed clearly within the context of complex interrelationships.

Cummins is not alone in his pleas for wider accountability.   Besides prejudice reduction, Banks (1995) notes that an empowering school culture and social structure are another of the five dimensions of multicultural education.   It is clear that classroom teachers can't continue to be solely responsible for innovations in instructional materials and for new approaches to traditional subjects.

Though we can find in this chapter and throughout this book innovative examples of what teachers can and do accomplish on their own, the issues of diversity and multiculturalism cannot be adequately addressed through lesson plans and instructional units alone.  At the district, state, and national levels there needs to be a concerted effort to rethink school structures and  practices and the power and access issues implicit in them.  As evidenced by their questions, teachers are calling out for back-up support from the larger community as well as from their students' homes.  Perhaps this is where attention needs to be given to school reform efforts (Goodman, 1995), site-based management initiatives (Odden & Wohlstetter, 1995), and school/family partnerships (Elkind, 1995; Epstein, 1995).

And maybe in all of this we need to find the beat of empowering (Cummins, 1986), of Bamberger's enticing (1974), and of Noddings' caring (1995).  These are the notions that move schools and classrooms away from reliance on shoeboxes.  These are the notions that make shoebox kits obsolete in publishing houses.   These are the notions that transform schools from shoebox factories, busily sorting and labeling students, into noble institutions valuing the potentialities in each of its students and the tasks to unfold them. These are the notions that dignify complexity, power reform, and move mountains.   These are the notions that empowered these teachers to create their own responses to their own questions, and to tailor their responses to the unique demands of their own settings and "children."  These are the notions that make redundant such unanswered teacher concerns as:  What's the big deal anyway?  Why has this become such an issue?  What about the teachers who don't want to deal with these issues?  Why are we, 'educated countries,' the only ones focusing on this when it is not something discussed in all countries?

Maybe it's the meaning of it all that we've lost sight of.

Maybe not.  Maybe I'd just made a slip in that teacher in-service presentation, pure and simple.  Shoebox...soapbox.  Maybe I'd been looking down, noticed my shoes were muddy, said shoebox, meant soapbox, and that was that.  No more, no less.

Maybe.

Maybe not.

## Overview of the structure and contents of the chapters that follow

In each of the chapters that follow, you will meet teachers of all levels of experience who share their backgrounds, dilemmas, and instructional innovations. Each of these individuals has come to multicultural education with some interest, though perhaps not complete agreement about what it is, why to do it, or how. They share their examples with you as an attempt to inspire you to create your own responses. Their work is intended to open up conversations about our own professional diversity of responses to the issues of multiculturalism. Their lessons are meant to exemplify the tremendous variation that can exist in our classrooms as we attempt to come to grips with the increasing demands, challenges, and opportunities which diversity presents. Their stories are meant as a way for you to participate in the process of putting theory into practice. You are invited to use any and all of what they have done to correspond with us about it (my e-mail address is deb@snowhill.com), to critique it, better it, springboard from it. Bagin, Gallagher, and Kindred (1994), in their textbook concerning school and community relations, state that, "Educators must stop fighting among themselves and start building coalitions" (p. 5). This book is meant to initiate the building of a coalition between academics and practitioners with the intention of empowering each other, enticing communities of support to join us in creating caring coalitions for children and the world. Join us in that spirit.

Chapters Two through Seven contain the curriculum units designed by the teachers described in Chapter One. Each of these chapters begins with a theoretical introduction to the lessons in the unit that follows. In these introductions the teachers present the sources, ideas, and perspectives they used in order to create the unit, and share the theory they attempted to align with their classroom practice. Following the theoretical introduction, a scope and sequence chart is presented in each chapter in order to provide the reader with an overview of what the unit lessons contain. Sample lessons follow the scope and sequence chart and contain objectives, time frame, materials, procedures, and assessment ideas as well as materials the reader may use as models for classroom use. Some chapters include homework ideas, letters to parents, extension activities, and/or notes concerning an issue or opportunity the lesson presents. Each chapter ends with a summary and implementation suggestions from the teacher as well as his/her personal profile. References and assessment ideas are contained in separate appendices at the end of the book.

Chapter Two is a language arts unit designed for second graders which focuses on preserving family histories. A proponent of whole language, Joan has woven reading, writing, speaking and listening opportunities throughout the lessons. There is a strong focus on the home-school connection in the homework letters which accompany the unit. Children in the early elementary school years can enjoy the experience of preserving their own stories with counting ropes, quilts, and storytelling connections to the literature Joan shares with them.

Chapter Three is a celebration of celebrations.  Designed for fourth graders, the lessons are alternatives to the traditional Halloween, Christmas, and Easter classroom "festivities."  Kelly presented her students with an opportunity to explore masks, instead of the ghosts and goblins to which some parents objected.  Her focus enriches the curriculum by offering art, theater, drama, music, and learning about other cultures.  Her mask unit was thoroughly tested on her fourth graders, but Kelly regrets her inability to "test" either the Christmas or Easter alternatives before this book went to press.  She encourages readers to test them out in their own classrooms (the unit adapts well to a broad range of grades) and share with us the knowledge and experience gained.

Chapter Four is an in-depth study unit of Japan created for gifted first and second graders.  The unit is a good model of how a single country and people can be shared with young children.  It is quite popular these days to have school-wide "multicultural fairs."  Usually these events include a number of countries (which may or may not be represented within the student body) and focus exclusively on food and music.  Mickey's unit does that and much more.  She refused to leave Japan "embedded" in the past, as many such units do by leaving children with the impression that kimonos and chopsticks are almost all there is to the Japan of today.  She also connects the children to the Japanese American experience as well.  It is a "tricky" issue with children so young. But Mickey's treatment of internment camps is as gentle as she is and suggests that we need not avoid such topics with our students.

Chapter Five is a blend of multicultural education and science for fourth graders.  What a combination!  Too often multicultural connections are confined to the language arts arena.  Tina refocused her meteorology unit from the physical science text adopted by the district to include the connection between climate and culture.  Her lessons incorporate "expert reports" on major weather conditions, in-depth studies of a particular country or region, and legends and myths from a variety of cultures which explain the natural phenomena the students are studying.  She also makes an important connection to the present by introducing global issues of deforestation, ozone depletion, and global warming.  This unit clearly shows that refocusing, though not easy, can be extremely rewarding for all concerned.

Chapter Six takes the multicultural connection into the social studies area with a group of sixth graders who are studying the primary documents of the United States. In this unit, Barbara expands the scope of the lessons to "give voice" to perspectives denied by those documents, those of women, African Americans, and Native Americans.  It is a fascinating journey into America's past and reveals both the strengths and the weaknesses of our country's heritage.  Math, role play, music, reading, writing, and art are all integrated into this social studies unit in a way that is a model for "across the curriculum" planning and organization.

Chapter Seven stays within the realm of social studies by providing a unit of study on the ancient Mexican civilizations of the Maya and Aztecs.  California curriculum guidelines mandate the study of ancient civilizations in the sixth grade.  Despite a statewide Mexican American population of over 50 percent, the guidelines do not include any study of that heritage. Karen remedied that oversight in her own classroom with a series of lessons that explore the same facets of the ancient Mexican civilizations that are presented in the standard curriculum on Egypt and Greece. Each lesson balances background information with hands-on activities in the areas of reading, writing, math, art, and/or music. Unfortunately, after designing the unit (for use the following year), Karen was transferred from sixth grade to Kindergarten. The lessons have been adopted in varying degrees by her former colleagues, but Karen hopes that some readers will take this to heart, as she did, and make it their own.

Chapter Eight is unique in that it does not contain any lessons at all. The chapter begins with a theoretical introduction in which Doug summarizes key points from the literature as guidelines. Rather than providing lesson plans, Doug has created four sections which contain selected bibliographies that follow those guidelines. The sections represent four major "cultural conglomerates" in our nation: African American, Asian American, Native American, and Mexican American. The bibliographies are not meant to be exhaustive, rather they illustrate the process of selection. Doug has included supplemental materials by noting filmstrips, videos or movies that complement the literature. Doug hopes that the readers will use his work as an example of classroom literature to share and have on hand for students to enjoy.

The Assessment Appendix at the end of the book contains rating scales, tests, checklists, rubrics, and so on, which correspond to the lessons in a particular chapter. Not all the chapters have assessments for the lessons. For the early elementary grades, most assessments are contained within the lessons themselves. When independent assessment instruments were utilized, they can be found in the Assessment Appendix as well. The upper grade units in social studies and science (Chapters Five, Six, and Seven) utilized multiple forms of assessment. The assessment procedures in the lessons direct the readers to the appropriate page of the Assessment Appendix, when necessary.

The Reference Appendix at the end of the book contains detailed reference information for each of the chapters. If a book is mentioned somewhere in the lessons (be it professional literature or children's literature), the reader can find the particulars in the Reference Appendix under the author's last name. The references are categorized by chapter. For example, if the reader is interested in finding the publication details for a myth mentioned in Tina's meteorology unit, Chapter Five, it can be found in the Reference Appendix in the Chapter Five section under the author's last name.

## Personal Profile

When I was 16 or 17 years old my mother invited a female friend to the house for coffee. I can't remember the exact circumstances, but I do remember that the woman brought her two children. They were about 7 and 9 years old, a boy and a girl, and they were as bored as I was at having to "stand by" while our mothers chatted.

Earlier that day I had discovered a nest of baby mice in a garbage can full of grass clippings so I took the kids outside to have a look. They were fascinated. We spent a long time out there, looking and marveling and watching and talking. Eventually our mothers joined us, and the children's' mother remarked, in passing, that she hoped I was considering teaching as a profession. I had never considered it, but her remark stayed with me and eventually guided my choice.

It's been almost thirty years since that day. I have been in education for twenty-four of those years if you count the time I studied the field in undergraduate school. And how the years have flown! I've taught preschool, elementary school grades two through five, middle school Spanish and remedial reading, adult literacy, and masters and doctoral level courses in multicultural education, curriculum development, assessment of student learning, children's literature and dealing with sensitive issues in the classroom. I've taught in a Montessori setting, in public schools, in private schools, and in outreach settings. I've taught teachers in Colombia, South America, on the East and West coasts of the United States, and in Department of Defense sites in Germany and England. It's always been a challenge, it's always been a joy, and it's always been underpaid!

Though currently a consultant in Alabama, I was an assistant professor of education at United States International University in San Diego and Irvine, California, at the time when the idea for this book was born. It was there that I had the good fortune to work with some very talented and inspiring teachers who were struggling, as I still am, with working out the theory-to-practice issue. In the pages that follow, the reader will see the results of their efforts and "hear" about the problems they confronted while translating what they learned about multicultural education into the confines of classrooms, state curriculum frameworks, and state adopted textbooks. They responded to unique populations which ranged from the extremely diverse to the not-very-diverse at all, from gifted and talented youngsters to severely disabled adolescents. They teach in a wide range of settings from elementary to high school, from suburban to inner city settings. They bring a wide range of expertise to the classroom: from no experience at all to very experienced indeed. They are, I think, very much like you, the reader. Somewhere in these pages you will find someone who resembles you. I hope you will take his or her example and make it your own. Perhaps in telling their tales they can demonstrate that there is nothing remarkable or magical about multicultural education. Nothing, that is, except dedication and effort, something which these teachers possess and give in abundance.

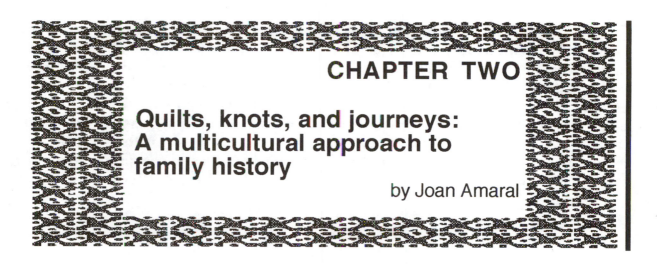

# CHAPTER TWO

## Quilts, knots, and journeys: A multicultural approach to family history

by Joan Amaral

The student population in today's classrooms is rapidly changing and becoming more diverse. Different ethnic groups are not "melting" into American society as was once thought to be the norm. Instead, groups are retaining customs, traditions, and languages of their native cultures and finding new pride in their heritage (Banks, 1991). Traditional classroom curriculum, methods, and strategies are not as effective as they once were thought to be. In order to engage students in learning, teachers must provide a relevant and meaningful curriculum.

Children's literature can be the catalyst that draws children in, captures their attention, and begins the process of developing tolerance, understanding, and ultimately, appreciation of the diversity that makes up our American society.

> Literature plays a strong role in helping us understand and value our cultural heritage as well. Developing positive attitudes toward our own culture and the cultures of others is necessary for both social and personal development. Carefully selected literature can illustrate the contributions and values of the many cultures. It is especially critical to foster an appreciation of the heritage of the ethnic minorities in American society.... Literature can contribute considerably toward our understanding and thus our respect (Norton, 1991, p. 2).

As teachers are well aware, parents are an important component of a child's development and education. Research has revealed that parents who actively support their children contribute more to their child's success in school than do those who provide passive support. The least effective parents, in terms of the child's ability to succeed, are those who are unsupportive. Parents must actively help, as well as encourage, their children to achieve (Berger, 1995, p. 4).

This instructional unit is an attempt to draw from the personal experiences of the children and their families. Through these personal experiences, children begin to build bridges between themselves and children of different ethnicities and cultures.

The unit consists of a collection of books portraying family histories and stories along with a curriculum guide of activities. It is designed to provide reading materials at the Second Grade level, however, it can easily be modified for use at First and Third Grade levels. The guide is arranged sequentially. However, the lessons may be used individually in any order. The goal is to encourage children to look beyond the physical characteristics of people to find commonalities in the human experience. Activities present family history to children through multiple perspectives. As children hear and read stories of families and examine their own family's experiences, they begin to see commonality in the diversity of family experiences.

 # Quick View Chart of the Instructional Unit

| Lesson One<br>The Patchwork Quilt | Lesson Two<br>The Josefina Story Quilt |
|---|---|
| In this week-long series of lessons, students read The Patchwork Quilt, learn about quilts as preservers of family history, and work together to create cooperative group friendship quilts. | In this seven-day series of lessons, students explore reading through The Josefina Quilt Story, continue to investigate their family histories, and create a story quilt which summarizes the events in the book. |
| Lesson Three<br>Knots on a Counting Rope | Lesson Four<br>Coming to America |
| Over the course of five days and through paired, choral, and call and response readings of Knots on a Counting Rope, students recreate the story by telling a childhood story about themselves, writing color poems, and reporting on how their names were given to them. | For an entire week, students enjoy a variety of stories about journeys to America which include: How Many Days to America; Angel Child, Dragon Child; Watch the Stars Come Out; and Grandfather's Journey. They continue to explore and share their family histories and themselves through interviews, letter writing, mapping, and mathematics. |

# LESSON ONE  THE PATCHWORK QUILT

Tanya becomes fascinated with the patchwork quilt her grandmother is making. As the seasons pass, each individual patch in the quilt takes on a special meaning and all the members of the family are represented in the quilt. When Grandmother becomes ill and can't work on the quilt, Tanya begins to work on the quilt by herself. Her mother and even her brothers help.

## Objectives:

- ☛ Students will identify the story elements of characters, setting, problem, and solution.
- ☛ Students will work together in cooperative groups to make a friendship quilt.
- ☛ Students will discuss ways that families preserve their histories.

## Time: One week

## Materials:

- ✂ Individual copies of The Patchwork Quilt
- ✂ Story book - 1 per student: made by stapling together 6 sheets of white paper
- ✂ Friendship quilt: 24" by 36" construction paper for backing
  6" by 6" white construction paper - 2 per student
  7" by 7" construction paper in assorted colors
- ✂ Homework Letter #1 (included on page 17)

## Procedures:

### Day 1

1. Discuss the origins of quilts and ask the children if they have quilts at home and who made them.

2. Introduce The Patchwork Quilt and read pages 1 to 7. Have the children identify the main characters. Have the children make the cover of their storybooks by writing the title of the book and the author on the top page. Have the children label the next page "Characters" and draw and label the main characters from the story.

3. Homework: Send home Homework Letter #1.

### Day 2

1. Share any quilts the children may bring from home and ask for their histories. Or share pictures of different kinds of quilts from books.

2. Reread the first 7 pages of the story. Read pages 8 to 15 with the children. Begin a time line to be compiled each day as you read. Have the children look for clues for the time line, for example, page 1: spring, page 8: August, page 9: Autumn and Halloween, and so on.

3. Have the children look through the book to identify the setting where the story takes place. Have them label the third page of their storybooks "Setting" and draw the setting of the story.

4. Tell the children that they will be working together in groups to make a friendship quilt. Give each child two pieces of 6" by 6" white construction paper. Each child will make two quilt blocks. On one 6" by 6" block they will draw a self portrait, and on the other block they will draw something they like to do. Have them complete both blocks. Tomorrow they will finish the friendship quilt in groups.

## Day 3

1. Continue to share quilt samples or pictures.

2. Recall what has happened in the story or reread the pages aloud. Tell the children that today they will read about a problem in the story. After reading pages 16 to 19, have the children identify the problem. Have them label the fourth page in their storybooks "Problem" and write about and illustrate the problem.

3. Next, ask the children to recall from the story the different patches in the quilt and the family members represented by those patches. Explain that today the children will work in groups of 6 to complete their friendship quilts. Everyone in the group will be represented in the quilt.

4. Pass out the quilt squares the children completed yesterday. First, the children choose two 7" by 7" pieces of construction paper for the borders of their quilt blocks. Next, they glue their blocks to the border squares. Divide the class into groups. In groups, the children agree on an arrangement of their quilt blocks before gluing them onto the 24" by 36" backing. Have them label their quilt. Give the children enough time to work through to a compromise as this is a difficult task at this age. Display the finished quilts.

## Day 4

1. Have the children reread the story orally with a "reading buddy." Pair a capable reader with a child who is less confident. The story can also be put on tape by a student, parent, or teacher for those children who need more practice before reading independently.

2. Review the characters, setting, and problem of the story. Finish reading the story and have students identify the solution to the problem. Children label the

fifth page of their storybooks "Solution" and draw and write the solution to the problem.

## Day 5

1. Go over the time line started on Day 2 and ask the children to recall the different patches added to the quilt in the story and the people the patches represent. Discuss with the children other ways that families preserve memories  (for example:  photographs, videotapes, scrapbooks, mementos, souvenirs of trips, and anything else of interest ).

2. Tell the children to label the last page on their storybooks "Memories."  On this page they will write or draw ways that their family saves memories.

3. This is a good opportunity to incorporate Patchwork Quilt designs and geometric shapes into the math lessons.  This idea extends the quilt theme to math and art and is a good way to continue through <u>The Josefina Story Quilt</u>.

## <u>Homework Letter #1</u>

Dear Parents,

We will be studying quilts as part of our unit on family history.  We will be reading about modern families and pioneer families and how quilts became keepsakes of family memories.  Please show your child any quilts your family may have and discuss their histories.  The class would love to see any quilts you would be willing to share with us. Please send them to school at any time this week.

We will be using quilts for math to explore fractions, geometric shape, and pattern.  In art we will be discussing the color wheel, primary and secondary colors, complementary colors, and combinations of colors and patterns used in quilt making.

If you have any quilting books, patterns, or pictures that you would like to share with us, please send them to school.

Sincerely,

# LESSON TWO

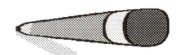

# THE JOSEFINA STORY QUILT

This is the story of a young girl, Faith, and her pet hen, Josefina, as the family travels west with a wagon train in 1850. There are problems and hardships to be dealt with along the way. Faith records the events of the journey in quilt blocks which eventually become the Josefina story quilt.

## Objectives:

☛ Students will create a quilt to retell the events in a story.
☛ Students will explore their family history.
☛ Students will orally retell the major events of a story.
☛ Students will discuss reasons why families move to new places.

## Time: 7 days

## Materials:

✄ Individual copies of The Josefina Story Quilt
✄ Six - 6" by 6" white construction paper per student
✄ An assortment of 18" by 24" colored construction paper - 1 per student
✄ Strips of chipboard 12" by 1"
✄ One diary per student - 8 to 10 pages
✄ Homework Letters #2 , #3, and #4 (included on pages 21, 22, and 23).

## Procedures:

### Day 1

1. Introduce the book and read the Author's Note on page 63. Ask the children why families might leave their homes and make such a long and difficult journey. Have the children turn to the Table of Contents and discuss the border used on this page. Turn to page 5 and point out to the children that each chapter has its own quilt block. Read the first chapter together to establish main characters, setting, and problem. Have the students work in groups of 2 or 3 to find three reasons Pa said Josefina couldn't go and three reasons Faith wants to keep Josefina. Have them decide if they think Josefina should go or not and tell their reasons for making that decision. Explain that families didn't have a lot of room in covered wagons for belongings and often had to leave behind cherished possessions. Have students write in their diaries about preparing to leave for California.

2. Next have children trace a 1" border around their 6" by 6" piece of white construction paper using the chipboard strips as guides. Have children choose symbols (no more than 3) to make a symbolic border around their quilt square - such as a feather to represent Josefina, a rocking chair to represent Ma, or a wagon wheel to represent the trip. Then have the

children draw a picture in the center of the quilt square to show something significant about Chapter 1.  Each day the children will follow this procedure to design their quilt squares.

3. Homework: Send home Homework Letter # 2.

## Day 2

1. Have children share information from Homework Letter #2.  Record answers on a chart.  Ask children to classify items that are similar and generate labels for each category ( example:  clothing, toys, entertainment, etc.).  Talk about which items would be necessities for a trip and which would be "nice to have" but not necessities.  Divide the class into small groups.  Have one child in each group write down the names of the categories on a sheet of paper.  Next have  the children tally the items in each category from their homework list of items they would take on a trip.  Then have the groups report back to the class and record their tally on a class chart.  Optional:  tell the children that there is less space for suitcases in the wagons than you thought.  Give them a number such as 1, 3, or 5 and have them individually or in small groups decide which items they would eliminate from their list as not absolutely necessary for the trip.

2. Review and discuss Chapter 1.  Tell the children that today they will read about Faith and her family beginning their trip to California.  Assign pages 15 to 28 to be read in pairs.  Students should be paired so less capable readers have a capable reader to assist them.   After reading the story children will write a diary entry either individually or in pairs.  If the children choose to work in pairs, each child should copy the story into his/her own diary.  Ask for volunteers to share their diary entries.   Next children design their quilt blocks for this chapter.

3. Send home Homework Letter #3.

## Day 3

1. Have children share information from Homework Letter #2.  On U. S.  or world maps, point out where families came from to reach the state where they live.  Ask volunteers to share reasons why their family moved to their state.  Discuss various modes of transportation and discuss why they would be chosen (Example:  cost, convenience, terrain to be traversed, etc.).  Optional:  make a class graph of the modes of transportation listed on the homework letters.

2. Discuss the chapter entitled "California, Ho" and read it aloud.  Turn to page 29.  Have the children predict what the trouble might be.  Assign pages 29 to 36 to be read in pairs.  Children write a diary entry and design a quilt block for the chapter.  Ask volunteers to share their diary entries.

## Day 4

1. Discuss and read aloud the chapter entitled "Trouble." A discussion of verbs fits well into this chapter as the children pick out the actions of the various animals involved. Ask the children to write or draw about a time when a pet caused a problem for them or their family. Children who do not have pets may pretend Josefina is their pet and make up a problem that she might create at their house. Have the children share their stories in small groups. Individuals may volunteer to share stories with the class. The stories can be bound into a class book and put in the library corner for students to read independently.

2. Assign the chapter entitled "The Rescue" to be read in pairs. Children write diary entries and design a quilt block for the chapter. Have volunteers read their diary entries.

## Day 5

1. Discuss and read aloud the chapter entitled "The Rescue."

2. In the chapter entitled "Robbers," the pioneers face different hardships. Before reading, brainstorm some possible difficulties encountered on the trip. Record answers and possible solutions. Ask the children how they think the Indians might have felt when so many new people were moving into the places where the Indians hunted and lived. Assign pages 46 to 54 for pair reading. After reading, children make a diary entry and design a quilt block for this chapter. Let volunteers read their diary entries.

## Day 6

1. Discuss and read aloud the chapter entitled "Robbers." Discuss with the children what it is like to lose a favorite pet. Assign the final chapter, entitled "Good-bye, Josefina" on pages 55 to 62. Children pair up and read the chapter, make diary entries, and design a quilt block.

2. Read outloud the The Quilt Story by Tony Johnson and Tomie dePaola. Compare and contrast the two stories with a Venn diagram.

3. Homework: Send home Homework Letter #4.

## Day 7

1. Have children share some of the things they learned from Homework Letter #4.

2. Read Wagon Wheels by Barbara Brenner to the class. Discuss the hardships faced by this pioneer family and their relationship with the Indians. Compare and contrast the Muldie family's experiences with Faith's family's experiences. Read the biographical information at the back of Wagon Wheels.

3. Today the children will assemble their story quilts. Children arrange and glue their quilt blocks onto an 18" by 24" piece of construction paper and label it, <u>The Josefina Story Quilt</u>.

4. In pairs, children retell the story of Josefina using their quilt to recall the important events in the story.

## Homework Letter #2

Dear Parents,

We are reading <u>The Josefina Story Quilt</u>, a book about a pioneer family that travels to California in a covered wagon in 1850. Since space is limited one of the decisions the family has to make is what to bring along and what to leave behind. Families often have to make this kind of decision when moving. Your child's job is to pack one large suitcase with necessities, such as clothes, shoes, jackets and their most cherished possessions. Children may list or draw the things they will include in the suitcase. Please return the "packed suitcase" with your child tomorrow.

Thank you.

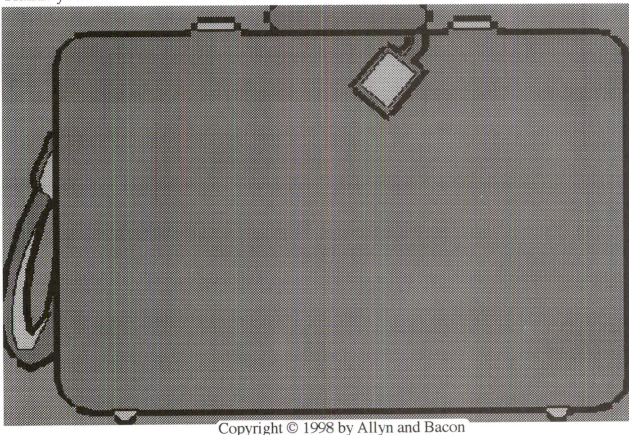

Copyright © 1998 by Allyn and Bacon

# Homework Letter #3

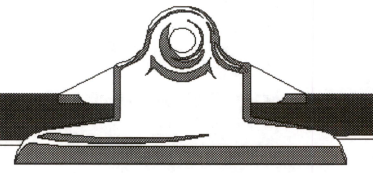

Dear Parents,

Today we read about a pioneer family starting out from Missouri and traveling to California in 1850 on a wagon train. In order to relate this story to personal experience, I am asking each student to find the following information about how his/her family moved to our state. Please help us.

When did your family come to our state?

_____
_____

From what city, state, or country did your family come?

_____
_____

How did your family travel to our state (car, boat, plane, wagon train)?

_____
_____

    Please feel free to include any other information that you think would be of interest to your child or our class about your family's migration here.

Please complete and return to school tomorrow.

Sincerely,

# Homework Letter #4

Dear Parents,

We have been reading stories about life "long ago." As an extension of our studies, your child will interview a parent or grandparent about what life was like for him or her as a child. Your child will want to know about similarities as well as differences between now and when you or a grandparent were a child. They will want to know what school was like, rules, chores, clothes, food, etc. Feel free to expand on the list and share whatever topics you think will interest your child.

Please help your child fill in the Venn diagram that is attached. Things that you did as a child (or a grandparent) go in the left circle. Things that your child does now go in the circle on the right. Things that you and your child have in common between then and now go in the middle where the two circles intersect.

I hope you and your child will find this to be a fun as well as informative activity. Please send it back to school on_____.

Sincerely,

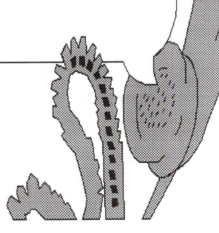

# LESSON THREE

# KNOTS ON A COUNTING ROPE

This book presents the oral tradition of storytelling used by many Native Americans. A boy and his grandfather share the story of events surrounding the boy's birth and the choosing of his name. Each time the story is told, a knot is tied in a rope until finally the boy knows the story by heart and can tell the story himself. Although the boy is blind, he sees his world through the vivid descriptions of his grandfather and participates in a horse race with the other boys at a tribal meeting.

## Objectives:

☞ Students will participate in choral reading to become familiar with written text.
☞ Students will work together in cooperative groups.
☞ Students will learn a personal story about themselves to share with the class.
☞ Students will use adjectives to describe colors.
☞ Students will learn the personal/family significance of their name.

## Time: 1 week

## Materials:

✄ Individual copies of Knots on a Counting Rope
✄ String
✄ Homework Letters #5 and #6 (included on pages 26 and 27).

## Procedures:

### Day 1

1. Language Arts: For the first reading of this book, gather the children in a circle, as if sitting around a campfire. If possible, dim the lights and simulate a campfire in the middle of the circle with some sticks or construction paper. Read Knots on a Counting Rope.

2. Homework: Children take home a brief description of the story (Homework Letter #5) and a piece of string. They are to learn a simple childhood story about themselves to share with the class. Each time a parent or family member tells the story, a knot is tied in their "counting rope" until they can finally tell the story themselves.

3. Math: Children can measure and cut their own counting rope strings for the homework assignment.

### Day 2

1. Reread Knots on a Counting Rope. This story works well for choral reading with a call and response pattern. Have the children read the boy's part and the

teacher can respond with the grandfather's answer. This also helps the children gain confidence with the text.

2. Grandfather uses senses other than sight to describe the world and colors to the boy. Have the students find and read Grandfather's and the Boy's descriptions of the sunrise, the sky, and the color blue. Ask the children to describe other colors using senses other than sight. Describe how a color might feel or sound. Record student responses to be used to write color poems. Children can use 4 or 5 of the responses to create a poem or make up their own color poems.

3. Homework: Send home Homework Letter #6.

## Day 3

1. Reread Knots on a Counting Rope in Buddy Reading Teams or in small groups. Individual students read the boy's part and the teacher or another student reads grandfather's reply. If children are comfortable with the text, they can do this in pairs and because it has already been modeled several times, they are usually successful with this technique.

2. Social Studies: Children will investigate how their name was chosen, whether their name has a special significance in the family, whether they were named for a relative, or whether their parents chose their name because they liked the sound of it or because it had a special meaning. Children can bring in books of names or the teacher can provide naming books for children to look up names and their meanings or histories.

3. Read Tikki Tikki Tembo by Arlene Mosel to the class.

## Day 4

1. Partner read Knots on a Counting Rope. Pair the capable readers with less capable readers. Students read the story together using the call/response pattern. Students should be familiar with the text by this time. If some students still have difficulty reading alone, allow them to read along while the more capable reader reads the story aloud.

2. Share with the class one or more of the stories from the book list (included in the Reference Appendix at the end of the book) and compare and contrast these to Knots on a Counting Rope using a Venn diagram or matrix.

## Day 5

1. Break the class into small groups. Each group gets a counting rope. When a child has the rope, it is his/her turn to tell his/her childhood story. As each child finishes the story s/he makes a knot in the counting rope and the rope is passed to the next storyteller until every one has had a turn.

2. Math:  Graph the number of knots on the individual counting ropes used for homework.  Have the children count the knots in their counting rope and make a class graph showing how many had three knots, four knots, five knots, and so on.

## Homework Letter #5

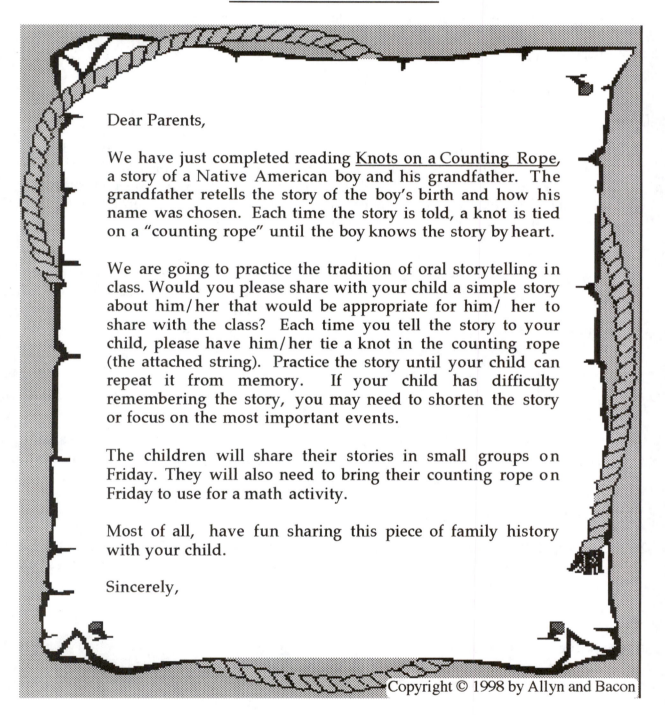

Dear Parents,

We have just completed reading <u>Knots on a Counting Rope</u>, a story of a Native American boy and his grandfather.  The grandfather retells the story of the boy's birth and how his name was chosen.  Each time the story is told, a knot is tied on a "counting rope" until the boy knows the story by heart.

We are going to practice the tradition of oral storytelling in class. Would you please share with your child a simple story about him/her that would be appropriate for him/ her to share with the class?  Each time you tell the story to your child, please have him/her tie a knot in the counting rope (the attached string).  Practice the story until your child can repeat it from memory.  If your child has difficulty remembering the story, you may need to shorten the story or focus on the most important events.

The children will share their stories in small groups on Friday. They will also need to bring their counting rope on Friday to use for a math activity.

Most of all, have fun sharing this piece of family history with your child.

Sincerely,

# Homework Letter #6

Dear Parents,

In <u>Knots on a Counting Rope</u>, a Native American boy learns how his name was chosen. Please help your child to learn about how his/her name. Some of the reasons for choosing names that we have discussed in class are: names with a special family significance; names of people who are special; and names that people like. The children will share with the class what they learn about how their name was chosen.

Also, if you have a baby naming book that you would be willing to share with the class, we would enjoy seeing it. Please send it to school with your child.

Sincerely,

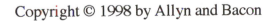

# LESSON FOUR

# COMING TO AMERICA

The United States is a nation of immigrants. People come to the United States from many different nations. These lessons focus on stories of how families arrive here and the difficult journeys some families have experienced.

## Objectives:

☛ Students will listen to and discuss the experiences of family journeys to America.

☛ Students will explore the countries of origin of their own family through family interviews.

☛ Students will share information about their family's country of origin.

## Time: 1 week

## Materials:

✂ Individual copies of titles: <u>Watch the Stars Come Out</u>, <u>Angel Child, Dragon Child</u>, <u>Grandfather's Journey</u>, <u>How Many Days To America?</u>

✂ Homework Letters #7 and #8 (included on pages 30 and 31).

## Procedures:

### Day 1

1. Ask the children "Where do Americans come from and how did they get here?" Discuss with the class that Americans come from all over the globe.

2. Explain to the class that sometimes families can't come to America all at once. Some members may have to stay behind until the family can send for them. Ask: Why do you think that is necessary? Read <u>Watch the Stars Come Out</u> to the class. As you read, ask the children to notice the details in the book's picture of life in the early 1900's. Ask: How is the girl like her Grandma? How is life different now than when Grandma was a girl? How would families feel being separated for months? How would the children feel traveling alone? How would they feel? Talk about the crowded conditions on the boat and the lack of things to do. Ask the children to pretend that they were traveling on the boat and ask them to write a letter to their parents telling about the trip. Ask volunteers to read their letters.

3. Homework: Send home Homework Letter #7.

### Day 2

1. Ask volunteers to share the countries of origin for their families and point them out on a world map.

2. Ask students to tell what they know about Vietnam and ask someone to find it on the map. Tell the class that you are going to read a story to them about Vietnam. Like the family in Watch the Stars Come Out, one member of the family has to stay behind in Vietnam until the family has enough money to send for her.

3. Read Angel Child, Dragon Child to the class. Using word and picture clues, ask the children to figure out how long it was before mother joined the family. Ask what is meant by Angel child and Dragon child. List on the board or a chart when Ut was an Angel child and when she was a Dragon child. Ask the students to make two lists: things they do when they are Angel children and things they do when they are Dragon children.

4. Art: Using a small school picture, children can make a little folded paper frame and a decorated envelope to give to a parent.

## Day 3

1. Discuss with the class that often times when families come to the United States, they still have family members in their country of origin. Ask the children if they have relatives in other countries and if they have visited them.

2. Ask the children to tell what they know about Japan and locate it on a map. If possible, show pictures of Japan, the landscape, cities, gardens, and houses. Read Grandfather's Journey to the class. As you read, ask the children to notice details in the pictures such as clothing styles and forms of transportation. Ask the children what the author means when he says "The moment I am in one country, I am homesick for the other."

3. Tell the children that they will interview a family member (or friend) from another country (or another state or area) to find out what it is like to live somewhere else.

4. Homework: Send home Homework Letter #8.

5. Art: There are many origami books available. There may be one or two children in class (or parents) who are familiar with origami if a teacher does not feel confident with the technique.

## Day 4

1. Ask the children to recall what the journey by boat was like in Watch the Stars Come Out. Tell them that today you are going to read a story about a different journey by boat. Read How Many Days to America? to the class. Ask: Who were the unhappy people who came to America long ago? How are these people like the Pilgrims? What are some of the reasons people leave their homes to look for new places to live?

2. Math: Provide catalogs or newspaper inserts showing clothing and toys (or ask students to bring them in). Tell the children that they may spend $50 to buy

new clothes and a new toy for the children in the story who had to leave most of their things behind when they left their home.  Let the children cut and paste their choices onto a piece of paper. Then they must write the prices and add them up. Remind them not to go over $50.

## Day 5

1. Today the children will share what they learned from their interview.  Allow them to share in small groups first.  Children with countries in common could be grouped together to share information.  Then groups can share what they found out with the class.

2. Make a class bulletin board with the information from Homework Letter #7.  Put each child's picture on the bulletin board arranging them around a world map.  Use yarn to connect each picture with the country or countries of origin.

## Homework Letter #7

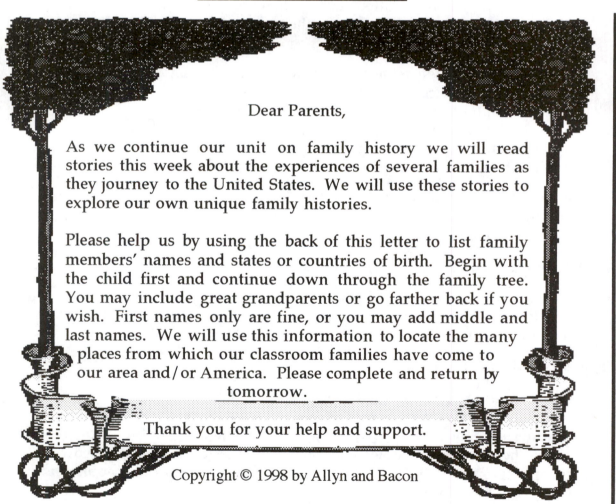

Dear Parents,

As we continue our unit on family history we will read stories this week about the experiences of several families as they journey to the United States. We will use these stories to explore our own unique family histories.

Please help us by using the back of this letter to list family members' names and states or countries of birth.  Begin with the child first and continue down through the family tree. You may include great grandparents or go farther back if you wish.  First names only are fine, or you may add middle and last names.  We will use this information to locate the many places from which our classroom families have come to our area and/or America.  Please complete and return by tomorrow.

Thank you for your help and support.

Copyright © 1998 by Allyn and Bacon

# Homework Letter #8

Dear Parents,

We have just finished reading <u>Grandfather's Journey</u> a story about a family with "roots" in two countries. Please help your child interview a family member who has lived in another country. If it's not possible to interview someone from another country, then another state or area would be fine. Please compare the two places with your child by completing this chart. Please return by

_____.

| | Name of state or country of origin of the person interviewed | United States (or name of our state) |
|---|---|---|
| **Size** | | |
| **Weather** | | |
| **Clothing** | | |
| **Transpor- tation** | | |
| **Holidays** | | |
| **Food/ Shopping** | | |
| **Language** | | |

## Summary and Suggestions

These lessons were developed to integrate subject matter and create opportunities in which all students can participate regardless of ethnic or cultural background. Family history, topic familiar to students and their families, becomes the springboard from which to explore the commonalities and differences of the human experience.

In the past, when I've used Knots on a Counting Rope, I found the repeated readings a benefit to the students in helping them with the rhythm and flow of the dialogue, the unfamiliar pattern of the print, and the challenging vocabulary. Through the call and response readings, children gain confidence and expression in their reading and are later able to enjoy reading the story independently.

In completing these lessons, I found them to be effective in involving all students in an examination of their own family's history as well as in looking at the experiences of others. Through these self-examinations, students began to see commonalities of experiences as well as differences. Children enjoyed relating and sharing their family stories with others. Often times these stories were a source of pride for the students, particularly when they related to the storybooks we shared in class.

The children enjoyed learning about their family history and sharing their families' stories. Motivation was high even for children who are somewhat shy. Parents expressed appreciation that the children were able to share information about their respective cultures. I also found that the range and variety of activities allowed for differences in learning styles and enabled all children to find a level of success.

In the future, I would like to expand upon the immigration unit to include stories of families coming by land from Latin American countries as well as stories of the origins of Native Americans. I would like also to find additional stories for the quilt unit that would include more variety in the cultures represented. In time, each of these units could be expanded to be a thematic unit. I am particularly interested in oral storytelling using artifacts such as the counting ropes, and I would like to investigate other cultures and artifacts such as storytelling dolls.

The books utilized in these lessons are a good beginning to a multicultural perspective on family history and the immigrant experience. The list of books is not exhaustive, however. Teachers utilizing the lessons will want to continue to look for additional titles that would extend and enrich the activities. There is a need for more immigrant stories dealing with those that came to America by land from Latin American countries and also a need for Native American stories of origin.

In addition, some of these stories may be available on videotape to supplement the books. Some teachers may want to tape record the stories for students who are auditory learners.

## Personal Profile

The school where I teach is located in Mira Mesa, California, within the city limits of San Diego. The school is a racially balanced and diverse Kindergarten through Fifth Grade elementary school.    In fact there is a 51 percent minority population in the school that includes Latino, Vietnamese, Filipino, and Chinese children.   My class this year has 20 students, the result of California legislation mandating a reduction in the class sizes in Kindergarten through Second Grades. It's a delight!!

I first became interested in multicultural education years ago when I pursued studies to obtain my Language Development Specialist (LDS) certification.   I was concerned at that time that I knew so very little about the children's backgrounds and the influences their cultures had upon their learning.  I wanted to learn more, and then I was "hooked."

Away from my second graders I love horses and own three of them.   Many of my free hours are spent with them.  Fortunately I live in the country in a small town outside of San Diego.  The commute is worth it for the peacefulness of the country and the serenity of riding through the hills and canyons nearby.  It is there that I gather my strength to meet the children's needs, and reflect upon the progress both they and I have made over the year. Multicultural education is a constant learning experience for everyone:  myself, the children, their parents, and the school.  My final word of advice would be to try it, enjoy it, and keep at it.  It's worth the effort!

# CHAPTER THREE

## Celebrations with a twist: Alternative lessons during Halloween, Christmas, and Easter

### by Kelly O'Hagan

The observance of Halloween, Christmas, and Easter creates a definite problem in public schools.  Many students in today's pluralistic society do not share the ethnic customs or religious convictions on which these holidays are based. The celebration of holidays in a "whole school" manner presents a conflict for these students. Additionally, some professional educators are beginning to question the appropriateness of public schools celebrating events which have obvious religious foundations.  Although avoiding the celebrations entirely may not be necessary, some alternatives would be helpful.  Currently available are "Holidays Around the World" thematic units.  However, these units are still religious in nature, may not cover the diverse cultures represented in the classroom, and do not do justice to their celebrations in either breadth or depth of presentation.

The need for an alternative holiday curriculum has arisen, in my opinion, for two reasons.  The first is the increasing amount of cultural pluralism and religious diversity present in today's classrooms. Secondly, parents and teachers are beginning to question the educational values of holiday festivities.  When public schools are being criticized for not providing students with the skills they need to enter the twenty-first century, can we afford to fill up valuable space in the curriculum with the Easter Bunny and Santa Claus?

These lessons were designed to increase the comfort level of all students in the classroom regardless of their religious or ethnic background.  The lessons are aligned with the Human Relations Approach to multicultural education, the goal of which is to develop positive interactions among students and between groups. Human relations activities aim to foster the self-esteem of each child.  The creative arts experiences provided in these lessons allow for a great deal of self-exploration. At-home extensions of the lessons encourage the learner to personalize concepts studied in class.  Additionally, the Human Relations Approach suggests that teachers utilize diverse strategies to actively involve the learner.  In this project, learners have the opportunity to create numerous artistic products.  They become familiar with the group process through cooperative learning activities.  Vicarious experiences in the form of literature, film, drama, and role-playing are also provided.  Some lessons require outside references to complete.  Please preview them carefully.

# Quick View Chart of the Instructional Unit

| Maskerade: A Halloween Alternative which explores multicultural masks | | |
|---|---|---|
| **Lesson One "Phantom of the Opera"** | **Lesson Two "Greek Comedy and Tragedy"** | **Lesson Three "Eskimo Laughing Masks"** |
| This introduction to the mask unit focuses on the music of the opera as students recognize feelings conveyed in the music, identify the reasons for wearing masks, and write a mask essay. | Students continue their study of masks by exploring comedy and tragedy masks as utilized in Greek theater. Children pantomime tragic and comic events in their own lives. | Students culminate the week-long unit with the construction of Eskimo laughing masks over a two-day period. The class holds a Laughing Contest on the final day. |

| Dollup: A Christmas Alternative which explores ethnic dolls | | |
|---|---|---|
| **Lesson Four "William's Doll"** | **Lesson Five "Molly's Pilgrim"** | **Lesson Six "Hopi/Zuni Kachina Cradle Dolls"** |
| The doll unit begins with identifying gender bias related to toys. Students learn the song "William's Doll" and discuss the implications for their own lives. | After reading the story of Molly's Pilgrim, students identify their ethnic heritage and design clothespin dolls to reflect their countries of origin. | Students continue their study and appreciation of the cultural role of dolls by creating Kachina Cradle dolls. |

| Eggstravaganza: An Easter Alternative which explores egg decorating | | |
|---|---|---|
| **Lesson Seven "Ugly Duckling Play"** | **Lesson Eight "Moravian Goose Eggs"** | **Lesson Nine "Polish Style Binsegraas Eggs"** |
| Students participate in a readers' theater rendition of the Danish folktale. | Students explore simple geometric shapes when decorating "slamenky." | The class decorates eggs with yarn. |

# LESSON ONE

# PHANTOM OF THE OPERA

The musical <u>Phantom of the Opera</u> takes place in the old Paris Opera House. Phantom, who hides his grotesque face behind a mask, falls in love with a beautiful actress named Christine. The title song from the soundtrack tells the story of their love. It will be used to introduce the concept of masks.

## Objectives:

☛ Students will recognize moods and feelings conveyed by the music.
☛ Students will identify several reasons why people wear masks.

## Time: 45 to 60 minutes

## Materials:

✂ <u>Phantom of the Opera</u> cassette tape or compact disc
✂ Tape/CD player
✂ Chart paper
✂ Markers
✂ Mask Essay and Rating Scale sheet (included on page 37).

## Procedures:

1. Give students background information about <u>The Phantom of the Opera</u>.

2. Play the title song from the soundtrack. Ask students to listen carefully to both the words and the music. Discuss the song with the students. Talk about the story it tells as well as how the students feel about the music.

3. Explain to students that Phantom wore a mask because he was embarrassed by his appearance.

4. Divide students into groups of four to think of other reasons that people wear masks. Pass out chart paper and markers. Brainstorm reasons for wearing masks, write ideas down on the chart paper, and share charts.

## Assessment:

Each student writes an essay addressing the topic of why people wear masks. Essays are evaluated using the Mask Essay and Rating Scale (on pages 37 and 205).

**MASK
PARAGRAPH**

Each student will write a paragraph (at least FIVE sentences in length) responding to the following topic:

## "Why People Wear Masks"

Paragraphs will be evaluated based on the following scale:

4       The response provides more than five statements supporting the topic. Sentences are clearly developed and convincing.

3       The response provides at least five statements supporting the topic. The sentences are somewhat clear but not convincing.

2       The response addresses the topic but is not developed sufficiently.

1       The response fails to address the topic and/or is poorly developed.

# LESSON TWO

# COMEDY AND TRAGEDY

Theater was an important tradition for the Ancient Greeks. Two important types of drama were comedy and tragedy. Comedies portrayed happy events, and tragedies portrayed sad ones. The masks that we readily associate with theatrical productions originated in ancient Greece.

## Objectives:

☛ Students will differentiate between comedy and tragedy.
☛ Students will dramatize comic and tragic events through pantomime.

## Time: 45 minutes

## Materials:

✂ A comedy mask (made or provided by the teacher)
✂ A tragedy mask (made or provided by the teacher)
✂ Comedy/tragedy quiz ( included on page 39)

## Procedures:

1. Introduce the concepts of comedy and tragedy. Define both.

2. Gather ideas from the class about comic and tragic events in their lives. Write the ideas on the board.

3. Show students the masks. Tell them that masks like these were first worn in ancient Greece many years ago. Point out Greece on a map.

4. Demonstrate a pantomime. Explain to students that volunteers will be pantomiming comic and tragic events.

5. Select volunteers for pantomimes. Let the volunteers wear one of the masks.

6. Allow audience to "guess" the pantomime.

7. Administer the quiz.

## Assessment:

A short quiz checks the students' understanding of the difference between comedy and tragedy (included on pages 39 and 206).

Name: _____

## Comedy/Tragedy Quiz

Decide whether each event is comic (C) or tragic (T). Circle the appropriate letter. *A total of 6 points is possible in this section.*

1.  You lose your favorite toy.                          C       T

2.  Your best friend moves away.                        C       T

3.  You see a funny movie.                              C       T

4.  You tell a great joke.                              C       T

5.  Your bike gets a flat tire.                         C       T

6.  You play a harmless trick on your teacher.          C       T

Tell about **two comic events** and **two tragic events** in your life. *A total of 4 points is possible on this section.*

Comic events in my life:

1.


2.


Tragic events in my life:

1.


2.

| Your score = | _____ |
|---|---|
| Possible points | 10 |

# LESSON THREE

# ESKIMO LAUGHING MASKS

Long ago the Eskimos held Laughing Contests. Participants wore funny masks, acted like clowns, and told jokes. The person who made the audience laugh the most was the winner.

## Objectives:

☛ Students will create Eskimo laughing masks.
☛ Students will simulate an Eskimo laughing contest.

## Time: 60 to 90 minutes

## Materials:

✂ Directions for constructing the Eskimo Laughing Mask can be obtained from The Kids' Multicultural Art Book (1993) by Alexandra Terzian
✂ 1 shoebox lid (per child in the class)
✂ 3 sections of an egg carton (per child in the class)
✂ 5 popsicle sticks (per child in the class)
✂ Scrap paper, markers, glue, scissors
✂ Decorative odds and ends such as feathers, buttons, felt, and ribbons.
✂ "At Home Extension" paper (included on page 42)
✂ "Here's what I thought" questionnaire (included on pages 53 and 209)

## Procedures:

1. Give the students some background information on Eskimo laughing masks. Show an example created in advance. Construct masks.

2. Hold a Laughing Contest in the classroom by allowing students to present their masks and by monitoring audience response (cheering, laughing).

3. Send home the "At Home Extension" paper (included on page 42).

4. Administer the "Here's what I thought" questionnaire (included on pages 53 and 209).

## Assessment:

The masks will be evaluated according to the Mask Rating Scale (included on pages 41 and 207).

# MASK
# RATING
# SCALE

1.  Decoration (A total of 6 points is possible)

    Presence of multiple features       (2 Points)     _____

    Variety of materials used            (2 Points)     _____

    Visual appeal                      (2 Points)     _____

2.  Creativity (A total of 6 points is possible)

    Characterization                (2 Points)     _____

    Color choice                     (2 Points)     _____

    Novelty                          (2 Points)     _____

3.  Neatness (A total of 6 points is possible)

    Proper use of glue and scissors       (2 Points)     _____

    Application of decorative materials    (2 Points)     _____

    Paint quality                     (2 Points)     _____

Your Score = _____
Possible points     18

# AT HOME EXTENSION

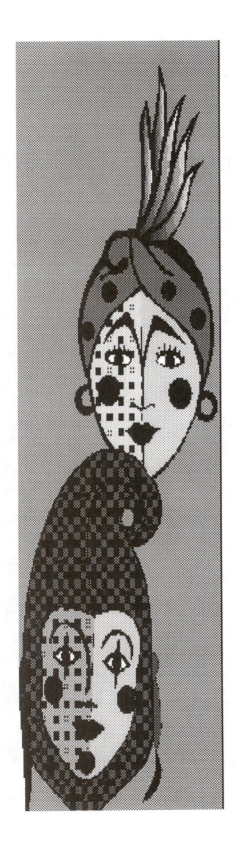

## A MASK OF ME

You will need a white paper plate. This plate will become your personal mask. You may cut it in any way you desire, or you may leave it round. Use household items to decorate the mask. The mask should reveal something special about you. Be creative and use your imagination. How can you represent yourself? What is something unique about you? What do you enjoy? What do you do when you are not at school?

Bring the mask back to school by the end of the week. There will be prizes for the most creative, unusual, and funny masks.

# LESSON FOUR

# WILLIAM'S DOLL

William's Doll is a story by Charlotte Zolotow and a song in the Free to Be You and Me collection conceived by Marlo Thomas. It tells the story of a boy who is teased because he wants a doll. It will be used to introduce the concept of dolls as universal playthings.

## Objectives:

☛ Students will begin to overcome gender bias related to toys.
☛ Students will recognize the universal importance of dolls as playthings.

## Time: 45 minutes

## Materials:

✂ A copy of William's Doll by Charlotte Zolotow
✂ Recording of "William's Doll"
✂ CD/Tape player
✂ Drawing paper, crayons, markers

## Procedures:

1. Read the story William's Doll. Play the music. Then sing it with the students, if possible.

2. Discuss the following questions about the story: Why was William teased? How do you think he felt? Why did he want a doll? How did William's grandmother help him? Have you ever been teased? How did you feel?

3. Ask girls to draw a picture of a "boy's" toy that they would enjoy playing with and ask boys to draw a picture of a "girl's" toy. Also have students write a sentence about why they like the toy.

4. Display drawings.

# LESSON FIVE

# MOLLY'S PILGRIM

Molly's Pilgrim by Barbara Cohen is the story of a young Jewish girl who is asked to create a pilgrim doll. Molly's Jewish pilgrim looks quite different from the traditional Thanksgiving ones. She is mocked by her classmates until her teacher validates her effort.

## Objectives:

☛ Students will recognize that individual differences should be respected.
☛ Students will identify their own ethnic heritage.
☛ Students will create a doll to represent their ethnic heritage.

## Time: 60 minutes

## Materials:

✄ A copy of Molly's Pilgrim by Barbara Cohen
✄ One clothespin per child
✄ Fabric scraps, scissors, glue, and markers

## Procedures:

1. Read Molly's Pilgrim to the class.

2. Discuss how Molly's pilgrim was different from the others and how Molly felt when her classmates teased her.

3. Explain to the students that America is a pilgrim nation. Many people can trace their family history back to a pilgrim from one country or another.

4. Have students identify their country of origin. Students can take this opportunity to research the clothing from that country, if the teacher wishes.

5. The students now design clothespin dolls representing their heritage like Molly did in the story.

## LESSON SIX

## HOPI / ZUNI KACHINA CRADLE DOLLS

The Hopis and Zunis of Arizona believed the Kachinas (spirits) would bring water and help the crops grow. Kachinas took many forms, including animals and people. Kachina dolls were often hung by a baby's cradle.

## Objectives:

☞ Students will understand the importance of spirits to Native Americans.
☞ Students will create Kachina cradle dolls.

## Time: Two 45 minute sessions

## Materials:

✄ Directions for constructing the Kachina cradle dolls can be obtained from The Kids' Multicultural Art Book (1993) by Alexandra Terzian
✄ A toilet paper roll for each child
✄ A 2 inch ball of aluminum foil for each child
✄ Papier mâché paste (recipe included in "Procedures")
✄ Newspaper strips (1 or 2 inches wide)
✄ 3 small feathers per child
✄ Tempera paint and brushes
✄ Acrylic gloss enamel
✄ Tape and glue
✄ "At Home Extension" (included on page 46)
✄ "Here's what I thought" questionnaire (included on pages 53 and 209)

## Procedures:

1. Give students some background information about Kachina dolls. Have a real Kachina doll to display or show them pictures of actual Kachina dolls.

2. Make Kachina dolls.

3. Papier mâché is made by mixing a 1/2 cup of flour with 3/4 cup of water in a small bowl until smooth and runny.

4. Send home the "At Home Extension" paper (included on page 46).

5. Administer the "Here's what I thought" questionnaire (included on page 53).

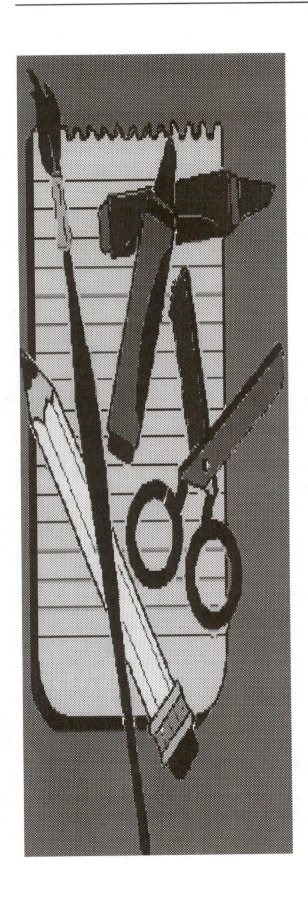

# AT HOME EXTENSION

## MY DOLL

Using things that you find around your home, create your own doll. You may use a sock, clothespins, old dishsoap bottles, or whatever else you can find or discover. See if you can design a doll that will tell something about yourself.

Just as you did for the homemade mask, be creative and use your imagination. How can you represent yourself? What is something unique about yourself? What do you enjoy? What do you do when you are not at school?

Bring the doll back to school by the end of the week. There will be prizes for the most creative, unusual, and funny dolls.

# LESSON SEVEN

# UGLY DUCKLING PLAY

<u>The Ugly Duckling</u> is a Danish folktale. It will be used in readers' theater form in order to introduce eggs and to explore the concept of beauty.

## Objectives:

☛ Students will identify many creatures that come from eggs.
☛ Students will appreciate beauty in many forms.
☛ Students will make cut-outs of beautiful creatures that come from eggs.

## Time: One hour

## Materials:

✄ A copy of <u>The Ugly Duckling</u> script from <u>Readers' Theatre for Beginning Readers</u> (1993) by Suzanne Barchers
✄ 8 1/2" by 11" tagboard, one for each student in the class
✄ Construction paper in a variety of colors
✄ Scissors, one for each student in the class
✄ Glue
✄ Markers, colored pencils, and crayons

## Procedures:

1. Assign parts for the readers' theater.

2. Read through the play.

3. Discuss the concept of beauty as presented in the story.

4. Distribute the tagboard and construction paper. Have the students brainstorm a variety of creatures that come from eggs. Using classroom reference materials or their own imaginations, have the students make paper cut-outs of the creatures they have identified and the egg shapes from which they are born. Glue the creature cut-outs onto the tagboard interspersed with the egg shapes to create collages.

## Assessment:

Products will be evaluated using the Egg Rating Scale (included on pages 51 and 208).

# LESSON EIGHT

# MORAVIAN GOOSE EGGS

In Moravia, goose eggs are decorated with straw shapes such as triangles, diamonds, circles, and squares. The decorated eggs are called "slamenky."

## Objectives:

☛ Students will design Moravian goose eggs.
☛ Students will explore patterns that can be made with geometric shapes.

## Time: 2 hours

## Materials:

✂ 8 1/2" by 11" tagboard egg shapes, one for each student in the class
✂ Construction paper in a variety of colors (shape master is on page 49)
✂ Scissors, one for each student in the class
✂ Glue
✂ Markers, colored pencils, and crayons

## Procedures:

1. Brainstorm questions the students have about Moravian goose eggs, and then send them on an information scavenger hunt. Using classroom reference materials or the library, students can try to locate the answers to their questions (either alone, in partners, or in group teams of three or more).

2. Regroup in 45 minutes to share the information with each other as a whole class activity (save a record to use with Lesson Nine).

3. Now is a good time to review patterning as the alternation of color and form (in this case). Students should be familiar with the criteria for evaluation of their egg patterns.

3. Have the students design and make Moravian goose egg patterns. Using the construction paper shape masters, students cut out the shapes and arrange them on their tagboard egg shapes. When the patterns are fully designed, students glue the construction paper shapes to the tagboard.

## Assessment:

Products will be evaluated using the Egg Rating Scale (included on pages 51 and 208).

# EGG SHAPE MASTER

# LESSON NINE

# POLISH STYLE BINSEGRAAS EGGS

The Polish people have their own unique way of decorating eggs which utilizes yarn. This lesson may be used to compare and contrast Moravian and Polish techniques, traditions, and meanings.

## Objectives:

☞ Students will explore the Polish tradition of egg decorating.
☞ Students will design Polish style Binsegraas eggs.
☞ Students will further explore patterns related to color and texture.

## Time: 2 hours

## Materials:

✄ Blank paper and colored pencils for each student
✄ One blown egg per student (have extras available)
✄ Yarn of various textures and hues
✄ Scissors
✄ Glue or rubber cement
✄ Q-tips
✄ "At Home Extension" paper (included on page 52)
✄ "Here's what I thought" questionnaire (included on pages 53 and 209)

## Procedures:

1. Utilizing the brainstormed questions about Moravian goose eggs, ask the students if they have any new questions about Polish Binsegraas eggs. Add these questions to the list, and then send the students on another information scavenger hunt.

2. Regroup in 45 minutes to share the information as a whole class activity. Complete a Venn diagram about the similarities and differences between the two traditions.

3. Discuss design as the arrangement of color, form, and texture (in this case). Have the students review the criteria for evaluation of their eggs.

4. Students should experiment first with color and swirl patterns on paper using colored pencils before they attempt to use yarn. Holding the blown egg in one hand, each student applies glue or rubber cement with a Q-tip and then arranges the yarn on the egg following the design.

5. Send home the "At Home Extension" paper (included on page 52).

6. Administer the "Here's what I thought" questionnaire (included on pages 53 and 209).

## Assessment:

Products will be evaluated using the egg rating scale (included below and on page 208).

---

# Egg Rating Scale

**Project:** _____

## Components:

| | | |
|---|---|---|
| 1. Designs (color, form, texture, and so on) | 2 points possible | _____ |
| 2. Neatness (cutting, painting, gluing, and so on) | 2 points possible | _____ |
| 3. Creativity | 2 points possible | _____ |
| 4. Visual Appeal | 2 points possible | _____ |
| 5. Color Choice (variety, vividness, and so on) | 2 points possible | _____ |
| | Student Score = | _____ |
| | Total Possible Points = | 10 |

**Name:** _____   **Date:** _____

---

# AT HOME EXTENSION

## 𝕸𝖄 𝕭𝕰𝕬𝖀𝕿𝕴𝕵𝖀𝕷 𝕰𝕲𝕲

You will need a blown egg* or another egg form (paper egg, clay egg, whatever you can imagine).  Using items available at your house, decorate your egg in the most imaginative way that you can.  **You may <u>not</u> use traditional Easter egg dye.**

Prizes will be awarded for the most beautiful, creative, and funny eggs.

* If you decide to use a blown egg, an adult should help you.  Using a pin, poke holes in both ends of a raw egg.  Blow through one hole until the egg yolk and white come out the other hole.  BE CAREFUL:  This is tricky and eggs are very fragile.

## Here's what I thought!!!

1. This project was:

2. I liked it because:

3. I didn't like it because:

4. I'm proud of my work because:

5. If we did this again, I would:

6. I learned that:

7. Additional comments:

## Summary and Suggestions

Before the book went to press I'd only had time to implement the Halloween alternative lessons. The major strength of these lessons was that the children truly enjoyed them. They looked forward to "mask time" each day. Students were able to express their identities and demonstrate their creativity in a non-threatening environment, and they liked doing it.

The projects were also well-received by the parents. Of the parents who were normally quite concerned about Halloween, not one objected to the mask lessons. They appreciated the multicultural and artistic values of the lessons; a shift from the traditional Halloween festivities in which they saw little educational merit.

The lessons also met the goal of promoting cultural awareness in the students. Many of them stated on their questionnaires that they learned that masks had different significance around the world. They were able to broaden their concept of masks beyond trick-or-treating.

The lessons apparently offer a worthwhile alternative to traditional, mainstream Halloween, Christmas, and Easter celebrations. They could be improved by incorporating a more interdisciplinary approach. Perhaps some additional social studies content could be included regarding the places and people who used the masks, dolls, or decorated eggs. For example, as the students study Greek comedy and tragedy, the lessons could expand to include a study of ancient Greece and its dramas. Math skills such as measuring and patterning could also be stressed during the lessons. The lessons are a good starting point for the inclusion of a multicultural approach in the classroom.

## Personal Profile

Currently I teach in a fourth grade at McKinley Elementary School in Corona, California. McKinley is a year-round school with an ethnically diverse population of nine hundred students in Kindergarten through grade 6. In addition to being a teacher, I have served as the P. T. A. president and vice president as well as advisor to the yearbook committee, student council, and drama club. I was named Corona-Norco's "Teacher of the Year" by the Wal-Mart Corporation in 1996.

My interest in multiculturalism began at a young age. As the only child of a corporate executive, I traveled extensively during my childhood, including several trips overseas. I have also moved frequently--six states from coast to coast in my twenty-nine years of life. I feel that these experiences have made me sensitive to the unique needs of each child in my classroom.

In my opinion, multiculturalism isn't something you do just once or that comes as a surprise in a classroom. It's the way life is. I try to represent life in its fullest in every way that I can.

# CHAPTER FOUR

## Domo arigato:
## A study of Japan,
## its people, and culture

### By Mickey Shannon

This unit on the people and culture of Japan was developed specifically for my class of gifted first and second grade students. I was taking a course in curriculum design for a masters' degree in multicultural education. At the same time, two parents actively involved in our PTA had taken on the task of providing a school-wide multicultural experience in which all students and teachers could participate. Second grade was assigned the continent of Asia and the four teachers involved chose to focus specifically on the country of Japan. It seemed to be the perfect opportunity to organize an in-depth study of Japan as a curriculum project for my coursework and to become fully involved with my students in our school's multicultural event.

My goal was to include art, music, the flag, geography, population, celebrations, literature, homes, food, education, language, numbers, clothing, and history. Through studying the similarities and differences of our two cultures, I hoped my students would gain an understanding of and a respect for another group of people. Singing, doing art projects, eating new foods, learning about holidays are activities we traditionally include in any study of another culture. Including historical and biographical lessons provides a depth to the unit which would otherwise be lacking. For example, the internment of people of Japanese descent during World War II is a difficult issue, but one to which children can relate. It is possible for them to imagine leaving their home, neighborhood, friends, toys, and pets. Perhaps they have had real experiences of leaving something or someone they loved to go to a new place. Given a safe classroom environment, most students are not only willing, but eager to share their own experiences from which they can make connections to those Japanese children going to relocation camps so long ago. These lessons provide the basis for discussion of complex social issues.

In first and second grade classes, I still have many students who are "learning to read," as well as those who are at the "reading to learn" stage. It has been my experience that reading information from a non-fiction book at an appropriate level provides a foundation of facts with picture connections for those emergent readers. That is the reason why most lessons begin with a read-aloud section. The books are then always available for beginning readers to look at illustrations and/or buddy read, and for stronger readers to explore other parts of the text for more information. The bibliography, included in the References Appendix at the end of the book, contains both required reading (necessary for one or more of the lessons) and optional materials (helpful to round out the students' experience).

# Quick View Chart of the Instructional Unit

| Lesson One<br>"Introduction" | Lesson Two<br>"Sakura" | Lesson Three<br>"What a country!" |
|---|---|---|
| In this lesson the children are introduced to Japan through what they know and want to know about it. | Children learn to sing "Sakura" (The Cherry Bloom Song) bilingually and practice the steps to a ribbon dance. | Geography is the focus in which the children construct a flag, and identify Japan, its islands, and bodies of water. |
| Lesson Four<br>"Population facts" | Lesson Five<br>"Art forms" | Lesson Six<br>"Celebrate!" |
| In this lesson the population is explored through discussion and playing a population game. | The class studies Japanese art by creating brush paintings and by folding origami. | The class is introduced to Japanese holidays and completes a flying carp art project. |
| Lesson Seven<br>"Haiku" | Lesson Eight<br>"Home sweet home" | Lesson Nine<br>"I'm hungry" |
| The class pursues its study of Japan through the creation of Haiku. | Children study the items in a Japanese home and make a "shoji." | Food is the focus and the class practices using chopsticks. |
| Lesson Ten<br>"Speaking and writing" | Lesson Eleven<br>"Itchy knee?" | Lesson Twelve<br>"Literature" |
| Japanese words and symbols are learned by making a dictionary and writing. | Children practice reading, saying, and using numbers in Japanese. | A folk tale is read, studied, and recreated by the class. |
| Lesson Thirteen<br>"History" | Lesson Fourteen<br>"Biographies" | Lesson Fifteen<br>"Pack it all together" |
| The class explores some of the ancient and recent history of Japan. | Children are introduced to four famous Japanese Americans who have contributed to our society and culture. | By creating a suitcase to hold their work and a passport to document their "travels" in Japan, the children conclude their study of Japan. |

# LESSON ONE  INTRODUCTION

## Objectives:

☞ Students will read and discuss the letter of introduction to the unit.
☞ Students will take the letter home to their parents.
☞ Students will recall facts they know about Japan and how they know them.
☞ Students will ask questions to which they would like to find answers as we proceed through the unit.
☞ Students will become excited, involved, enthusiastic, and motivated to learn about Japan.

## Time: 1 - 2 class periods

## Materials:

✄ Letter to parents (included on page 58)
✄ Two large sheets of butcher paper
✄ Marking pens

## Procedures:

1. Pass out one letter to each student.

2. Read and discuss the letter together. Students may suggest items they know they can bring for the class "Japan Center."

3. Students put the letter in their backpacks to go home.

4. As students recall facts they know about Japan, write the facts and how the students know them on the butcher paper chart titled "What We Know."

5. As students ask questions about Japan, write the questions on the butcher paper chart titled "What We Want to Know."

6. The two charts should be displayed in the classroom throughout the unit.

## Note: As students bring items for the Japan Center, you may want to take time that day for the student to share the item with the class and discuss any special rules for handling the item. Some items may be placed in the room for display only. Some items may be placed in plastic food storage bags labeled with the item and student's name.

Dear Parents,

In the weeks ahead our class will focus on a study of Japan and its people. The students will examine objects from everyday life in Japan and use the spoken and written language from that country. They will learn about the art, literature, and music of Japan. In order to make this a hands-on experience, we need your help in providing the following items from Japan: books, magazines, newspapers, toys, money, kitchen items, school supplies, clothing, tapes of music, songs, stories, musical instruments, slides or videos, chopsticks, rice bowls, chopstick rests, uncooked rice, green tea, dried pressed seaweed, noodles, sweets, rice crackers, lunchboxes, calligraphy brushes, ink, pencils, pencil boxes, maps, postcards, paper fans, cushions, and paper lanterns.

We welcome guest speakers (parents, relatives or friends) who have traveled or lived in Japan and anyone who has a related experience or even a favorite Japanese recipe to share.

As parents, you enhance your child's learning by visiting the library to find out more about Japan and by going to a Japanese restaurant or market. If you haven't already, try eating a family meal with chopsticks!

Thank you for your interest and support !

# LESSON TWO  "Sakura"

## Objectives:

☛ Students will memorize the Japanese and English words to the song "Sakura".
☛ Students will learn a simple ribbon dance.
☛ Students will perform the song and the dance for parents and/or other classes.

**Time:** A few minutes each day until the performance

## Materials:

✀ A copy of the words for the song "Sakura" (words to the song are included on this page, and dance instructions are included on page 60)
✀ A recording of the music for practice and performance
✀ Two tongue depressors per student
✀ Two pink and two white 2" by 24" tissue paper streamers per student
✀ Stapler

## Procedures:

1. Practice melody and words in English and Japanese to the song "Sakura" each day.

2. When the song has been well-learned, begin practicing the ribbon dance adding one section at a time.

3. Staple a white and pink streamer to each tongue depressor. You may want to make practice ribbons for a dress rehearsal.

4. To perform the dance, students wear a white shirt or blouse with dark pants or skirt. Students hold one ribbon in each hand.

5. Perform the song and dance for an audience.

### "Sakura"
### Cherry Blossom Song:
### An Ancient Japanese Folksong

Cherry blossom, cherry blossom / Sakura, Sakura
Gently swaying in the air / Ya- Yo- i no so- ra- wa
Sweet the fragrance everywhere / Mi- wa- ta- su ka- gi- ri
Petals soft and colors bright / Ka- su- mi ka ku- mo- ka
Floating clouds that seem to say / Ni- o- i zo i- zu- ru
Come and see, Come and see / I- za- ya, I- za- ya
Come and see the cherry blossom / Mi ni yu- ka- n

# Ribbon Dance Instructions

1. Student stands with legs apart, arms straight out at sides, a "ribbon" in each hand.

   A. "Cherry" While leaning slightly to the left, student brings right hand over head in an arc to meet left hand which remains still.

   B. "blossom" Body returns to center as right hand moves straight across front of body, returning to original position.

Repeat for:

| A. "Cherry" | A. "Gently" | A. "in the" |
|---|---|---|
| B. "blossom" | B. "swaying" | B. "air" |

2. Student should be in the original stride position.

   A. "Sweet the" Student brings right hand straight across the front of body to meet left hand which remains still. Student's feet stay in open stride position, but pivot slightly to left.

   B. "fragrance" Student returns to original position by bringing right hand straight across front of body. Feet pivot back to face straight ahead.

   C. "Every" Student arcs both arms up, hands meet over head and continue down until pointing straight down.

   D. "where" Arms open out to original position.

Repeat for:

| A. "Petals" | B. "soft" | C. "and colors" | D. "bright" |
|---|---|---|---|
| A. "Floating" | B. "clouds that" | C. "seem to" | D. "say" |

3. Student should be in the original stride position.

   A. "Come and see" Student steps out on left, then right, then left foot. Meanwhile, arms arc inward, circle once, then 1/2 circle and arms end crossed with hands on opposite shoulders.

   B. "Come and see" Student steps back on left, back on right, then back together with left. Meanwhile, arms arc down from crossed over chest position, circle once, then 1/2 circle and arms extend out to side.

4. Student should be in the original stride position.

   A. "Come and" Student swings arms together left. Student shifts weight from side to side as arms move from left to right.

   B. "see" Student's arms swing together to right.

Repeat for:

   A. "the cherry"
   B. "blossom"

5. Student arcs hands over head and bows.

# LESSON THREE

# WHAT A COUNTRY!!

## Objectives:

☛ Students will make a flag of Japan.
☛ Students will label the Pacific Ocean and the four main islands of Japan.
☛ Students will locate Japan on the globe.

## Time: 1 - 3 class periods

## Materials:

✄ A globe
✄ One piece 9" x 12" white construction paper for each student
✄ One piece 5" x 5" red construction paper for each student
✄ Several tagboard circle patterns
✄ Pencils, scissors, glue
✄ Activity paper "Japan," showing the four main islands (included on page 62)
✄ Books: <u>A New True Book JAPAN</u>, <u>Journey Through Japan</u>, <u>Japanese Americans</u>

## Procedures:

1. Show students the globe. Review what a globe is. Review what an island is. Point out Japan and the Pacific Ocean in relation to where they live.

2. Read and discuss: <u>A New True Book JAPAN</u>, pages 4 - 9, <u>Journey Through Japan</u>, page 6 and pages 20 - 27, <u>Japanese Americans</u>, page 6.

3. Students trace circle pattern onto red construction paper. Cut. Glue red circle to center of white construction paper. The flags make an attractive border for a Japan bulletin board.

4. Students complete the activity paper by coloring and labeling the islands and identifying the surrounding bodies of water.

**Note:** As students are working, call up one or two students at a time to show you Japan, the four islands, and the Pacific Ocean on the globe as part of a performance assessment.

# Japan:  What a country!!

Cut out the names and label each of the four main islands and surrounding bodies of water of Japan.  Then follow directions to complete the paper.

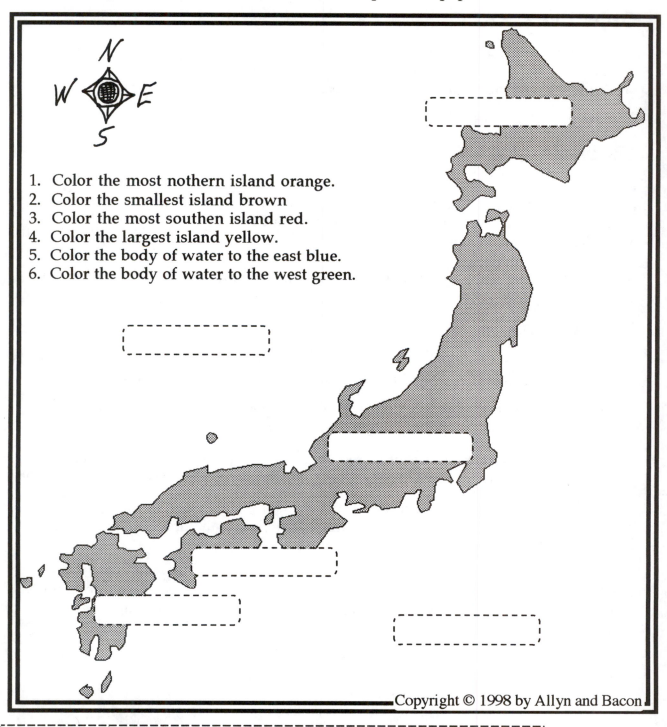

1.  Color the most nothern island orange.
2.  Color the smallest island brown
3.  Color the most southen island red.
4.  Color the largest island yellow.
5.  Color the body of water to the east blue.
6.  Color the body of water to the west green.

| HONSHU | SHIKOKU | HOKKAIDO | KYUSHU |

| PACIFIC OCEAN | SEA OF JAPAN |

# LESSON FOUR  POPULATION FACTS

## Objectives:

☛ Students will gain awareness of the density of Japan's population and how that contributes to the attitudes and customs of the Japanese people.

## Time: 1 class period

## Materials:

✂ Masking tape
✂ Books: A New True Book JAPAN, pages 10, 11, 17 - 19; Japan: The People, pages 1 through 9; Journey Through Japan, page 28; Japan World Neighbor Series, pages 15 and 28

## Procedures:

1. Read aloud and discuss A New True Book JAPAN, Japan the people, and Journey Through Japan. See above page numbers.

2. Japan and California are similar in size but very different in population, as this activity will illustrate. Play the Population Game (instructions follow "Procedures").

3. Discuss Japanese customs as described in Japan World Neighbor Series, page 28. How does Japan's dense population affect the way people treat each other?

---

## Instructions for the Population Game

1. Using masking tape, create a 3 foot by 6 foot area to represent Japan and California.

2. Select two students to represent the population of California. Have them stand, walk, recline, and move around in the area you have created with tape.

3. Now have ten more students join these two. Have them stand, walk, recline, and move around in the same area.

4. Discuss and compare the two experiences with the class. What was it like with only two students? What was their experience when twelve students moved in the same space?

---

Based on material from "This Place is Crowded" by Vicki Cobb. Copyright © 1992 by Vicki Cobb. Published by Walker and Company. All Rights Reserved.

# LESSON FIVE  ART FORMS

## Objectives:

☛ Students will have the opportunity to see prints of Japanese art.
☛ Students will gain an understanding of the importance of art to the people of Japan.
☛ Students will create Japanese art by making a brush painting on a scroll and by folding origami.

## Time: 3 class periods

## Materials:

✄ Pictures or prints of Japanese art, if available
✄ Books:  A New True Book: JAPAN, Journey Through Japan, Japanese, Japan: Traditions and Trends
✄ Two tongue depressors for each student (spraypainted black), 6"x9" white construction paper, black tempera paint, brushes
✄ Origami paper, or xerox paper cut into squares
✄ A book of origami instructions such as: Origami in the classroom (Vols. 1 and 2) (1965) by Chiyo Araki or Folding Stories:  Storytelling and Origami Together (1991) by Petrell Kallevig.

## Procedures:

1. Show and discuss Japanese pictures or art prints, if available.

2. Read aloud and discuss A New True Book: JAPAN, pages 42, 43; Journey Through Japan, page 30; Japanese, page 43; Japan: Traditions and Trends, page 55.

3. Students use 6"x9" white construction paper and black tempera paint to create a Japanese brush painting.  They should select a subject from nature, such as a flower or a butterfly.  Tell them to use a relatively dry brush, place their subject in the center of the paper, and use light, feathery strokes.  Students glue one tongue depressor to the top of their painting and one at the bottom to create a scroll-like effect. Use a hot glue gun and black yarn to affix a loop to the top tongue depressor for hanging the painting.

4. Students create origami art.  Choose a project appropriate for your students' age and ability.  If parent volunteers are available, they can work with two students at a time.  Provide paper for students to practice during free time.

# LESSON SIX  CELEBRATE!

## Objectives:

☛ Students will learn about several Japanese holidays and how they are celebrated.
☛ Students will make a flying carp art project.

## Time: 1 - 2 class periods

## Materials:

✄ Books: <u>A New True Book: JAPAN</u>, <u>Japanese</u>, <u>Japan: World Neighbor Series</u>
✄ Several tagboard patterns of the carp (included on page 66)
✄ Two pieces of 12"x18" construction paper for each student in assorted colors
✄ Paper clips, pencils, scissors, glue
✄ Crayons, markers, and/or paint
✄ Five 1"x12" tissue paper streamers for each student in assorted colors
✄ One or two pieces of 9"x12" newsprint or newspaper
✄ Hole punch, yarn

## Procedures:

1. Read aloud and discuss <u>A New True Book: JAPAN</u>, page 34; <u>Japanese</u>, page 46; <u>Japan: World Neighbor Series</u>, page 29.

2. Students select two sheets of construction paper. Paper clip the two sheets together. Trace around the tagboard pattern. Cut. Students should be reminded to keep the paper clips in place so that the two sides of the fish are identical.

3. Without removing the paper clips, fish can be decorated with crayons, markers, paint or a combination of these. One side or both may be decorated. The teacher should demonstrate various ways to add scales, fins, eyes, lips.

4. Tissue paper strips are glued to the inside of the tail so that they will be hanging down when the two sides are glued together.

5. The two sides of the fish are glued together, leaving an opening at the mouth.

6. One or two sheets of newsprint are used to lightly stuff the fish.

7. Punch a hole through both sides of the fish at the center of the mouth. Tie a loop of yarn through the hole for hanging. The fish are attractive hanging from the ceiling during the unit.

## THE FLYING CARP
(Enlarge pattern onto  12" x 18" tagboard)

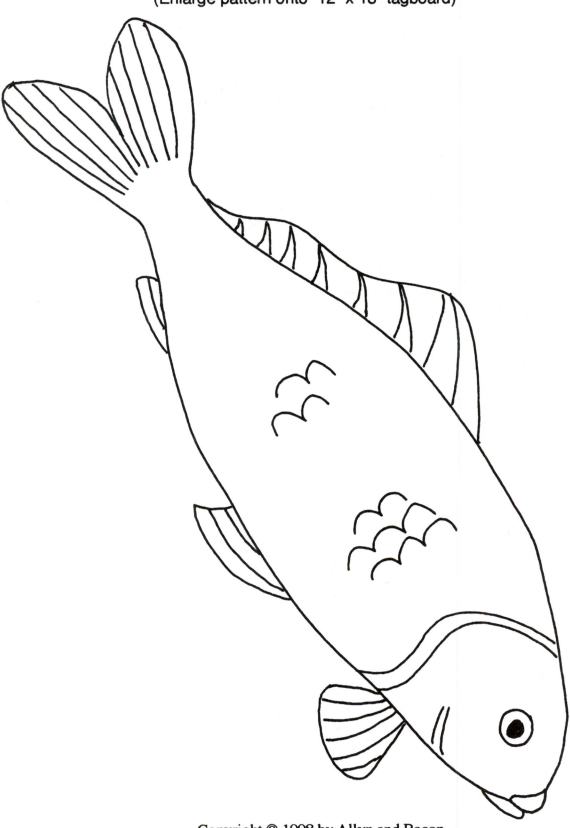

# LESSON SEVEN

# "HAIKU"

## Objectives:

☛ Students will divide words into syllables.
☛ Students will create a Japanese Lantern Poem and/or a Haiku Poem.

## Time: 1 or more class periods

## Materials:

✂ Examples of Haiku poetry.
✂ Japanese lantern pattern (included on page 68)
✂ 9"x 12" red construction paper
✂ Tagboard lanterns, slightly larger than the lantern pattern (to be used as backing)

## Procedures:

1. Discuss syllables. Say various words and clap the number of syllables in each.

2. Explain that a Japanese Lantern Poem consists of 5 lines, a one syllable word in the first line, two syllables in the second line, three syllables in the third line, four syllables in the fourth line, and one syllable in the last line. The topic is usually something beautiful or found in nature. The poem gets its name from the shape the words take as they are centered on the page.

3. Brainstorm with students vocabulary they might need and create a word bank together. Occasionally stop and ask how many syllables are in a given word. Create a class Lantern Poem together. Demonstrate how to center each line.

4. Students write a rough draft. Check syllables, centering, spelling, topic, and title. Students copy their poem onto the lantern paper. Students trace the lantern pattern onto the red construction paper. Cut. Glue or staple poem to tagboard backing for display.

5. Explain that a haiku is a three line Japanese poem about nature with 5 syllables in the first line, 7 syllables in the second line, and 5 syllables in the third line. Brainstorm vocabulary and create a class model. Students create their own poem. Students may use 6"x6" white construction paper and watercolor paints to create a watercolor illustration of their haiku. The poem can be recopied or typed by an adult onto 5 1/2"x 8 1/2" paper. Fold a 9"x 22" sheet of green or blue tagboard evenly into thirds horizontally, creating a standing triangle. (The face of each side of the triangle is approximately 7 1/2" by 9"). Staple to secure. Staple the poem to the front of the triangle and the illustration to the back.

**Note:** For a combination first/second grade class, first graders created the Lantern Poem and second graders created haiku.

# Japanese Lantern Pattern

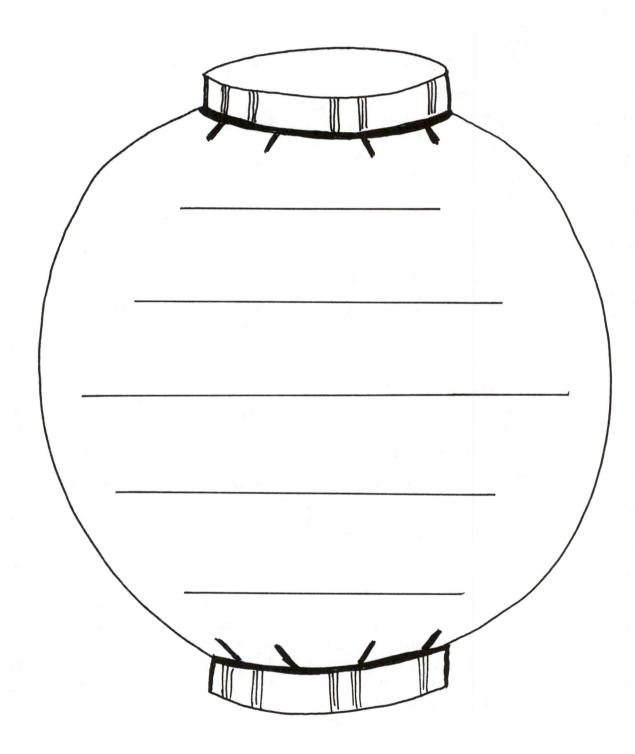

# LESSON EIGHT

# HOME SWEET HOME

## Objectives:

☛ Students will learn the names for items in a traditional Japanese home.

☛ Students will gain an understanding of the importance of neatness, order, and respect for privacy in the Japanese home.

## Time: 2 class periods

## Materials:

✄ Books: <u>A New True Book: JAPAN</u>, <u>Japan: The People</u>, <u>Japan: Traditions and Trends</u>, <u>Japan: World Neighbor Series</u>

✄ Information sheet "The Japanese Room" for each student (included on page 71)

✄ Activity sheet "The Japanese Room" for each student (included on page 72)

✄ One 9"x 12" piece of red tagboard for each student

✄ Two 3"x 12" pieces of black construction paper

✄ One 5"x 8-1/2" piece of white xerox paper for each student

✄ Crayons, pencil, ruler, scissors, stapler

✄ One popsicle stick for each student

## Procedures:

1. Read aloud and discuss <u>A New True Book: JAPAN</u>, pages 20-24; <u>Japan: the people</u>, page 10; <u>Japan: Traditions and Trends</u>, page 49; and <u>Japan: World Neighbor Series</u>, page 21.

2. Read aloud and discuss the information sheet describing the different items found in the Japanese home.

3. Students color the Japanese room, adding some things they think might be found on the table. Add beautiful art work to the kakemono.

4. Staple the finished room to the red tagboard.

5. Each student folds two black strips of construction paper in half lengthwise. The strips should be placed across the front of the tag mounted room so that the fold of the top strip is even with the top of the red tagboard, and the fold of the bottom strip is even with the bottom of the red tagboard. The strips will extend beyond the edges of the room. At the right side of the room, fold 1" of the strips to the back, and staple the strip to the back of the red tagboard, leaving the section of strip on the front free. Do this to both the top and bottom strip. At the left side of the room, move the edge of the tag slightly toward the center of the strips so that there is 1" of strip extending beyond the left edge. This will make the strips shorter than the length of the room, the

room will curve, and the project will stand on its own.  Staple the strips to the back of the left side.

6. Students use white xerox paper to make a shoji (screen).  Holding the paper vertically (5" side across the top, 8 1/2" edge down the side), demonstrate how to use a ruler and pencil to mark off five one-inch increments down the left side and the right side. Then lay the ruler across the marks to draw a straight line. Students should draw five straight lines horizontally across the paper. Repeat across the top of the paper and the bottom line to draw straight lines down. Students should now have a grid of squares on the top half of the screen.  If this is too difficult for younger students, it can be dittoed ahead of time for them or omitted.

7. Students outline the pencil lines with black crayon or marker. Center the popsicle stick lengthwise on the left side of the screen as a door pull/handle.  Glue. The popsicle stick can be omitted.  Or, another stick can be added to the right side for strength as the screen is pulled from either side.

8. Insert the top of the screen into the top black strip in front on the right side of the room.  Insert the bottom of the screen into the bottom strip.  Students can now slide the screen back and forth across the front of the room.

# THE JAPANESE ROOM
## INFORMATION  SHEET

This is a drawing of a Japanese Room.  How is it like a room in your house? How is it different?

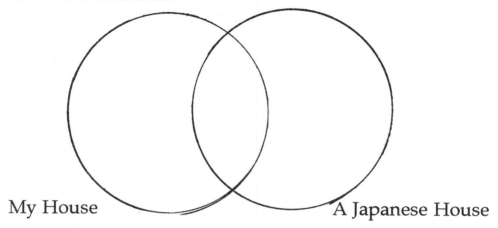

My House                    A Japanese House

The SHOJI is a screen that is covered with an opaque white paper.  It acts like a curtain since you cannot see inside the house when it is closed. However, light comes into the room through the SHOJI.  The wooden part of a SHOJI screen can be made out of natural unpainted wood to show the beauty of the wood.

The TATAMI is like a rug.  It is a mat made out of reeds tied together. They are a standard size and a room in Japan is measured by how many TATAMI are needed to fill the floor space.

The OSHI-IRE is the closet where the mattress (FUTON) is kept.  The Japanese people sleep on the FUTON on the floor and only take the FUTON out of the closet when it is time for bed.

The ZABUTON is a type of pillow that takes the place of a chair.  In a traditional Japanese home, the family kneels or sits on the ZABUTON on the floor.

The TOKONOMA is a special place in the house where art such as the scroll (KAKEMONO) and a flower arrangement (IKEBANA) is displayed.

# A JAPANESE ROOM

SHOJI

OSHI-IRE

ZABUTON

KAKEMONO

TOKONOMA

TATAMI

IKEBANA

# LESSON NINE 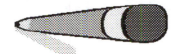 I'M HUNGRY

## Objectives:

☞ Students will note the similarities and differences between Japanese and American food.
☞ Students will experience Japanese food by tasting.
☞ Students will use chopsticks.

## Time: 1 class period

## Materials:

✄ Rice and rice cooker
✄ Plates, one for each student
✄ Chopsticks, one set for each student
✄ Markers (optional)
✄ Seaweed sprinkles, dried seaweed (optional)
✄ Books: <u>A New True Book: JAPAN</u>, <u>Japan: The People</u>, <u>Japan: Traditions and Trends</u>, <u>Japan: World Neighbor Series</u>

## Procedures:

1. Start cooking the rice in the rice cooker at the beginning of the lesson. Students can raise their hands as soon as they smell the rice.

2. Read aloud and discuss <u>A New True Book: JAPAN</u>, pages 25 and 26; <u>Japan: The People</u>, pages 12 and 13; <u>Japan: Traditions and Trends</u>, pages 45 and 46; <u>Japan: World Neighbor Series</u>, pages 22 and 23.

3. Pass out a set of chopsticks to each student. Students may use a marker to add Japanese characters or a nature design to the top of the chopsticks. For safety reasons, be sure design does not extend onto the area of chopsticks which will touch food.

4. When rice is finished, students can use their chopsticks to enjoy eating rice with seaweed sprinkles and dried seaweed.

# LESSON TEN

# SPEAKING AND WRITING

## Objectives:

☛ Students will learn pronunciation and meanings for a few simple Japanese words and phrases.
☛ Students will practice forming Japanese characters for a few words.
☛ Students will make a mini-dictionary.

## Time: 1 - 2 class periods, a few minutes each day

## Materials:

✄ Books: Japan: The People
✄ One mini-dictionary page for each student (included on page 75)
✄ Crayons, stapler
✄ Black markers
✄ Japanese writing page for each student (included on page 76)

## Procedures:

1. Read aloud and discuss Japan: The People, page 15.

2. Pass out the mini-dictionary page to each student. Read the words and phrases together. Practice the words and phrases a little each day with the class. Have them work in pairs or teams to learn the words together. Students cut out the pages and color them, if desired. Staple the pages together in order.

3. Students complete the "Japanese Writing" page with black marker.

4. If possible, have a Japanese language tape for the students to listen to and practice vocabulary.

# Japanese Mini-Dictionary

_____ 's
(name)

**Very Own**

**Japanese**

**Dictionary**

**Friendship Words**

Konnichiwa    Hello

Sayonora    Good-bye

Domo Arigato   Thank you

Dozo      Please

## Pets

| | |
|---|---|
| Inu | Dog |
| Usagi | Rabbit |
| Neko | Cat |
| Uma | Horse |

## Family members

| | |
|---|---|
| Okasan | Mother |
| Otosan | Father |
| Kyodai | Brother |
| Shimai | Sister |

## Size Words

| | |
|---|---|
| Ookii | Big |
| Chiisai | Small |
| Nagai | Long |
| Mijikai | Short |

## Useful Phrases

Kore wa nan desu ka.
  What is this?
Are wa nan desu ka.
  What is that?
Kore kudasai.
  Give me this one.
Misete kudasai.
  Show me please.

# Japanese Writing

There are three forms of writing in Japan.   One form is called Katakana. Katakana is mostly used to write foreign words. More commonly people use the second form of Japanese writing, called Hiragana.  It has fifty one letters that represent sounds like the English alphabet.   The third form of Japanese writing is called Kanji and it is a set of characters that represent ideas or  words.  In the boxes below are examples of Hiragana and Kanji forms of writing.  Practice writing in Japanese.  Which are Hiragana and which are Kanji?

| | | | |
|---|---|---|---|
| ぞど<br>Do-zo (Please) | ぞど | ぞど | |
| こねこ<br>Ne-ko (Cat) | こねこ | こね | |
| いがな<br>Na-ga-i (Long) | いがな | いがな | |
| 木<br>Tree | 木 | 木 | |
| 木木<br>Forest | 木木 | 木木 | |
| 雨<br>Rain | 雨 | 雨 | |

# LESSON ELEVEN

# ITCHY KNEE?

## Objectives:

☛ Students will make two counting books.
☛ Students will practice using Japanese numbers.
☛ Students will do two dot-to-dot papers with the numbers printed in Japanese.

## Time: 2 - 3 class periods

## Materials:

✄ Books: <u>Count Your Way Through Japan</u>
✄ One pre-folded, pre-stapled booklet of white construction paper for each student
✄ One "Counting in Japanese" paper for each student (included on page 78)
✄ A dot-to-dot paper for each student (included on page 79)

## Procedures:

1. Read aloud and discuss <u>Count Your Way Through Japan</u>.

2. Prepare the construction paper counting book ahead of time. For each counting book, cut 3 sheets of 9"x12" white construction paper. Fold the 9" edge of the first sheet down 3 1/2" and crease. Fold the second sheet down 4 1/2", crease, and slip it under the short flap of the first page. Fold the third sheet down 5 1/2", and slip it under the short flap of the second page. Place two staples at the top next to the fold. There should now be a 3 1/2" top page and 5 more pages, each one about 1" longer than the one before.

4. In black crayon, students print the title "My Japanese Counting Book" on the top flap. Students print the numbers 1, 2, 3, 4, 5 on the left side, one on each flap. Students print the Japanese word for each number on the center of each flap. Students draw the Japanese character for each number on the right side of each flap.

5. Students lift each flap, one at a time, and draw a picture of the corresponding number of items in crayon. For example, one Torii Gate on page one, two chopsticks on page two, three fans on the page three, and so on.

6. Pass out the dot-to-dot page. Students draw lines in pencil to connect the numbers in order. Color the pictures with crayon.

## COUNTING IN JAPANESE

| ENGLISH WORD | ENGLISH NUMBER | JAPANESE WORD | JAPANESE NUMBER |
|---|---|---|---|
| one | 1 | ichi | 一 |
| two | 2 | ni | 二 |
| three | 3 | san | 三 |
| four | 4 | shi | 四 |
| five | 5 | go | 五 |
| six | 6 | roku | 六 |
| seven | 7 | shichi | 七 |
| eight | 8 | hachi | 八 |
| nine | 9 | kyu | 九 |
| ten | 10 | ju | 十 |

Copyright © 1998 by Allyn and Bacon

# JAPANESE NUMBER DOT-TO-DOT

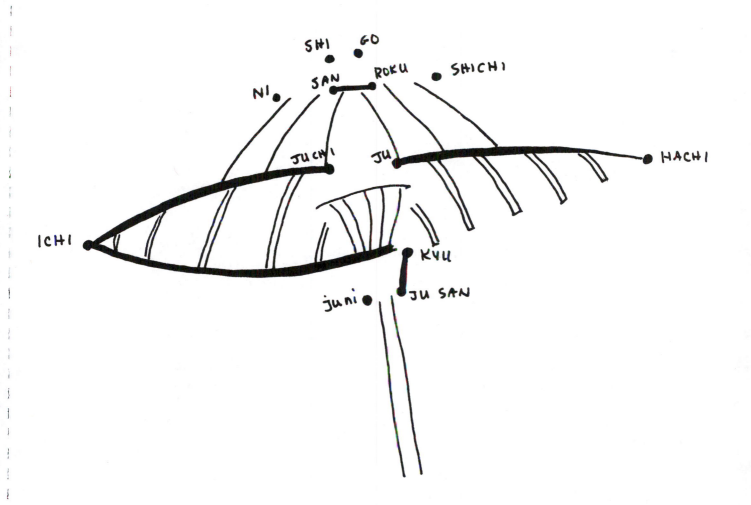

# LESSON TWELVE

# FOLK LEGEND

## Objectives:

☛ Students will become familiar with a popular Japanese legend.
☛ Students will practice capitalization and punctuation.
☛ Students will create a poem, chant, or song.

## Time: 1 class period

## Materials:

✄ Books: <u>Peach Boy</u>
✄ One "Momotaro, the Peach Boy" activity paper for each student (included on page 81)
✄ Paper, pencils

## Procedures:

1. Read aloud and discuss <u>Peach Boy</u>.

2. Pass out one activity paper to each student. Students complete the paper by correcting the capitalization and punctuation errors.

3. On a separate sheet of paper, students may create a song, poem, or chant about the hero of the village, Momotaro, and what he did for the people.

4. Allow time for students to share their poem, songs, and chants with the class.

**Note:** For students who are having difficulty getting started on their poem, song, or chant, the following is one possible strategy to "unblock" the writer. After the class has settled in and everyone is quietly thinking or writing, wait a few minutes and then ask for volunteers to stand and read aloud just what they have so far. It does not have to be finished or perfected, but this may help other students get over that initial block about what to write. Have a few students share, then ask everyone to continue writing. Do this several times during the writing period, so that a variety of students are able to share their work in progress. This takes only a few minutes and is not a time for criticism or suggestions. The teacher gives a positive comment and then calls on someone else.

# Momotaro, the Peach Boy
## Activity Paper

Try to recall what happened in the story as you answer these questions. You may look at the book to help you remember.

1. Why was the boy named Momotaro?

_____

_____

2. Why did Momotaro leave his village?

_____

_____

_____

3. Who were Momotaro's three companions?

_____

_____

4. How did the three companions help Momotaro?

_____

_____

_____

5. What did Momotaro bring back to the village?

_____

_____

6. Why is the legend of Momotaro still told in Japan?

_____

_____

7. Name three things about Momotaro that you liked.

_____

_____

_____

# LESSON THIRTEEN

# HISTORY

## Objectives:

☛ Students will gain a general understanding of at least 2 legends of how Japan was formed, what Shoguns and Samurai were, the opening of Japan's borders for trade, Japanese immigration to Hawaii, Japanese immigration to the U.S., W.W. II and internment camps, and redress.

## Time: 3 - 4 class periods

## Materials:

✄ Books: Japanese Americans
✄ Paper, pencil
✄ A Letter to the President of the United States (included on page 83)

## Procedures:

1. Read aloud and discuss Japanese Americans, pages 8, 11-25, one section at a time.

2. Students write a descriptive story in which they create their own island and then illustrate it.

3. Students write a letter to the President of the United States during W.W. II explaining why Japanese families should or should not be placed in internment camps.

**Note:** A good additional resource for teachers is "Home Was a Horse Stall" which first appeared in Teaching Tolerance in the Spring of 1995. This "story of intolerance" focuses on Japanese internment and is now available in the text component of the curriculum kit, "Shadow of Hate," available through Teaching Tolerance. Refer to the Reference Appendix for this chapter for more information.

# A letter to the President of the United States

# LESSON FOURTEEN

# BIOGRAPHIES

## Objectives:

☛ Students will learn about four famous U.S. citizens of Japanese ancestry.

## Time: 1 class period

## Materials:

✂ Books: <u>Japanese Americans</u>
✂ Paper, pencil

## Procedures:

1. Read aloud and discuss <u>Japanese Americans</u>, page 35 - Kristi Yamaguchi, page 36 - George Tsutakawa, page 37 - Lydia Minatoya, page 38 - Senator Daniel K. Inouye

2. Students write a paragraph about what they would like to pursue as a career when they are adults and why that interests them.

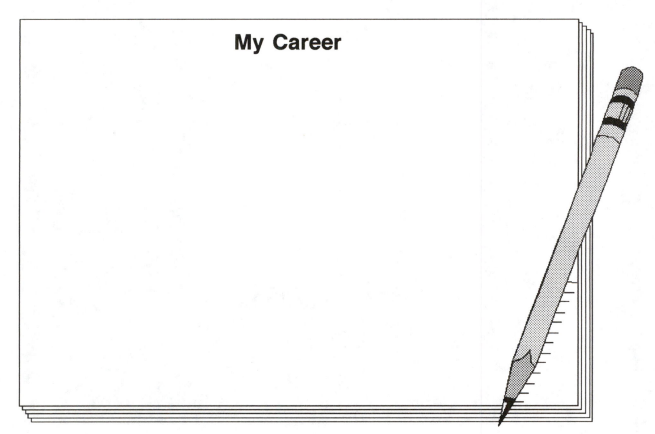

**My Career**

Copyright © 1998 by Allyn and Bacon

# LESSON FIFTEEN

# PACK IT ALL TOGETHER

## Objectives:

☛ Students will make a suitcase in which they can save their products from the unit.
☛ Students will design travel stickers which show the beauty of Japan.
☛ Students will make a passport.

## Time: 1 class period

## Materials:

✂ One 14"x 22" sheet of colored tagboard (red is a good choice) for each student
✂ Several tagboard suitcase patterns (see illustration in "Procedures")
✂ Three 4"x 6" white self-adhesive stickers for each student
✂ One 6"x 9" dark blue construction paper rectangle for each student
✂ One 1-7/8" self-adhesive gold seal for each student
✂ Three "Passport" papers for each student (included on pages 86, 87, and 88)
✂ Crayons, scissors, black markers, ink pad
✂ Optional - small 1"x 1-1/2" photograph of each student

## Procedures:

1. Fold the tagboard in half. Place the suitcase pattern on the tagboard with the bottom of the suitcase on the fold. Trace. Cut the sides and top. Staple the sides. The suitcase pattern looks like this:

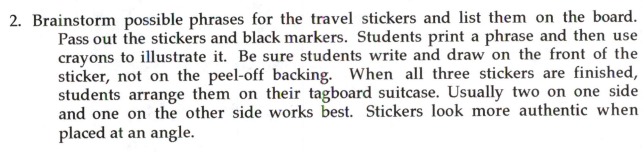

2. Brainstorm possible phrases for the travel stickers and list them on the board. Pass out the stickers and black markers. Students print a phrase and then use crayons to illustrate it. Be sure students write and draw on the front of the sticker, not on the peel-off backing. When all three stickers are finished, students arrange them on their tagboard suitcase. Usually two on one side and one on the other side works best. Stickers look more authentic when placed at an angle.

3. Students complete the "Passport" papers. Photograph of Bearer page may include an actual photo of the student, or students may draw their own face with crayons. Thumbprints may be made by using an ink pad. Students complete Travel Notes pages by writing some things they have learned about Japan during the unit or by writing as though they are actually traveling through Japan. Students cut out each page. Place pages in order. Fold the World Traveler sheet in half and place the cut pages inside. Fold the blue

construction paper in half to make the cover and place the pages inside. Staple along the left side.  Place a gold seal on the front cover of the passport and use black marker to write "United States Passport" around the seal.

**Note:**  These activities were two that my students enjoyed tremendously. The suitcase acts as a portfolio to collect the students' work for the unit.  This project comes at the end of the unit because students must experience the previous lessons in order to create phrases and illustrations on the travel stickers which represent the beauty of Japan. The suitcase may be made at the beginning of the unit, work can be collected and stored in it, then the stickers may be added at the end.  The suitcase may be made by the students or may be pre-made by parent volunteers.

## Passport Cover Sheet

PASSPORT

**United States
of America**

Copyright © 1998 by Allyn and Bacon

# PASSPORT NUMBER:

PEN AND INK ENTRY OF THE PASSPORT NUMBER BY THE BEARER

BEARER'S ADDRESS IN THE UNITED STATES:

_____

BEARER'S FOREIGN ADDRESS:

_____

IN CASE OF EMERGENCY NOTIFY THE INDIVIDUAL NAMED BELOW:

Name: _____

Address:

_____

_____

**The Principal of**

**_____ school**

**hereby requests**

**all whom it may concern**

**to permit this student**

**to pass without delay**

**and in case of need**

**to give help**

**as befits citizens of the**

**world.**

## Name:
_____

## Birthplace:
_____

## Birth Date:
_____

## Issue Date:
_____

## Expiration Date:
_____

## Signature:
_____

**Photograph of bearer**

**Left Thumbprint**      **Right Thumbprint**

| VISAS | | TRAVEL NOTES |
|---|---|---|
| Entries | Departures | |

## TRAVEL NOTES

## IMPORTANT INFORMATION

**THIS PASSPORT IS THE PROPERTY OF THE STUDENT. IT MUST BE SURRENDERED UPON DEMAND MADE BY AN AUTHORIZED REPRESENTATIVE OF THE BEARER OR HIS/HER TEACHER. IT IS NOT VALID UNLESS SIGNED BY THE BEARER ON PAGE 3.**

# Summary and Suggestions

Because of the difficulty in teaching two separate lessons in every subject to a combination class, I chose to do four in-depth units of study combining both Social Studies and Science with lessons appropriate for both first and second graders. We studied the ocean with a study of the Native Hawaiian culture. We studied mountains, forests, and meadows with a study of Native American people of those areas. We studied the polar regions by learning about the Inuit people. And we ended our year with the unit on Japan.

By the end of the year, three things happened which I had not expected. Occasionally, I have a student who, because of lack of training, lack of experience, or self-consciousness, tends to laugh at others who look or act differently, who are hurt, or who make mistakes. Over the course of the year, one such student became much more sensitive. He was able to stop and think before reacting and showed much more compassion and understanding for others.

During the unit on Japan in particular, I observed one of my students who is partially of Japanese ancestry as he developed a real sense of pride in this part of his heritage. I watched him very carefully at the beginning to be sure he wasn't embarrassed or feeling singled out. Other students were not aware of his ancestry, and I let him decide what, when, how, and especially if he would like to share with the class. At first, he seemed reluctant and unsure about discussing his heritage, although he did raise his hand to say he thought he might have a couple of things on our list to share in our Japan center. By the end of our unit, he was sharing almost every day about what he had learned about his Japanese culture and had volunteered his mother to come in to do a lesson for us. She spoke about her family, celebrations, and food. She brought chopsticks for each child, cooked rice in a rice cooker, and gave the students seaweed sprinkles and dried seaweed to try. The morning was a huge success! This student developed interest, pride, and enthusiasm in his own culture and ancestry over the course of the unit.

Lastly, I had the advantage of having my first graders the next year as second graders. As our school-wide multicultural event approached (we had been assigned Scotland this time), my returning second graders began telling the rest of the students all about the unit we had done the year before on Japan. I was amazed at their recall, understanding, and enthusiasm.

Although this unit was designed for a group of gifted students, it would be appropriate for any primary class, with modifications, as necessary. Through this unit, I hope that I have given my students the opportunity to solve problems, share ideas, create, and perform in fun, interesting, and challenging ways. I hope my students have gained in empathy and understanding, and I hope at their own level, they have discovered the value of cultural diversity, the importance of human rights for all people, and the necessity for respect for those who are different from ourselves.

# Personal Profile

I am currently a second grade Special Day GATE teacher at Valencia Elementary School in Laguna Hills, California in the Saddleback Unified School District. The school has about 860 students and is a magnet school for the GATE program in our district. Our school is predominantly Caucasian, with few African-American students, a small numberof Asians and a growing Hispanic population. There is a wide socio-economic range, from extremely wealthy to lower income families.

Aside from teaching, my main joy in life is spending time with my family and friends. There never seems to be enough of those special moments just being together. Those are the moments I enjoy most in my classroom as well as the times when we just seem to be together, sitting on the floor talking about life. That's when I find those teachable moments occur most often, and connections and insights can be made naturally.

As I have spent time working on my masters' degree in multicultural education, I have begun to look at things differently. How would another group of people react to what was said or done, or a particular television program or museum exhibit? I would hope that because of the time my students and I have spent together and the thoughts, ideas and feelings we have shared in the classroom, my students would also be out in the world seeing things differently and making a difference.

# CHAPTER FIVE

## How's the weather? Incorporating a multicultural approach toward meteorology

### By Tina Waters

Combining multicultural education and meteorology makes sense for two main reasons. First, all cultures are affected by weather and climate in an observable way. Second, by integrating the teaching of cultural diversity with a current "established" curriculum, students can see that multicultural education is a basic part of their education that permeates every part of their lives. It is not just something extra added on to the curriculum. Because of this format, and the fact that many lessons approach an issue from a perspective different from the mainstream culture of the classroom, the unit also reflects the Content Integration Model that James A. Banks advocates. In this model, ethnic studies are linked with global education. This is an important goal of the unit.

This unit has been designed to be used concurrently with the fourth grade meteorology unit that my school district purchased. However, the multicultural unit has been developed in such a way that it can compliment any meteorology unit with few adjustments. As the teacher, I have many important roles in the implementation of this unit. I need to blend the multicultural lessons with the district unit for meteorology. Also, I oversee the independent work that the unit requires, making sure that students have the resources they need to successfully study their region's weather and culture, and that there are a variety of cultures and regions represented.

This unit is designed to set an atmosphere of acceptance and understanding for different cultures in my classroom early in the year, and to give knowledge of different cultures as a starting point. The unit is also designed to offer students the opportunity to view problems from perspectives of different cultures and/or nations, and to introduce the students to the many ways culture influences a person's life. My hope is that by knowing other cultures and by learning about diverse perspectives, students will be able to see the great value of living in a diverse nation. In this respect, the unit reflects a Human Relations Approach to multicultural education.

 # Quick View Chart of the Instructional Unit

| Lesson One<br>"When the Wind Stops"<br><br>Students read When The Wind Stops, discuss culture, and create a student definition. | Lesson Two<br>"Forecasting the Weather"<br><br>Students learn to read weather reports, select a country or region to study, and read Cloudy With A Chance Of Meatballs. | Lesson Three<br>"Huichol Indian Culture"<br><br>After reading The Tree That Rains, students discuss Huichol culture and climate, and begin journals. |
|---|---|---|
| Lesson Four<br>"Weather Research"<br><br>Students read Weather and begin to research the weather in their chosen country/region. | Lesson Five<br>"Expert Reports"<br><br>The class reads Storm, and groups are assigned particular weather conditions on which to become expert. | Lesson Six<br>"Tornado!"<br><br>The class reads and discusses The Storm. The expert group on tornadoes reports and everyone makes a tornado. |
| Lesson Seven<br>"Snow and Thunder Storms"<br><br>Students compare three different cultures' tales about the origins of thunder and lightning. Expert groups report. | Lesson Eight<br>"Hurricane"<br><br>Expert groups report on hurricanes, monsoons, and typhoons. The class reads Hurricane. | Lesson Nine<br>"Mayan Culture"<br><br>Students read Rain Player and discuss the Mayan Culture in relation to droughts. Expert group reports. |
| Lesson Ten<br>"Inuit Culture"<br><br>Students read Houses Made Of Snow and Skin and Bones. Discussion centers on defending a thesis statement. | Lesson Eleven<br>"Culture vs. Climate"<br><br>Students locate and research aspects of culture influenced by climate for their particular region. Students present findings. | Lesson Twelve<br>"Ozone Depletion"<br><br>Students learn about ozone depletion, list causes, and identify what they can do to prevent further damage. |
| Lesson Thirteen<br>"Global Warming"<br><br>Students learn about global warming, list causes, and identify what can be done to prevent further damage. | Lesson Fourteen<br>"Deforestation"<br><br>Students locate rain forests, identify causes, and role-play multiple perspectives of the problem. | Lesson Fifteen<br>"Final Assessment"<br><br>Students take a unit exam and evaluate the multicultural meteorology unit. |

# LESSON ONE

# WHEN THE WIND STOPS

## Objectives:

☞ After listening to the story <u>When the Wind Stops</u>, students will list ways in which weather can affect people's lives.
☞ Students will discuss the definition of culture.
☞ Students will circle those aspects of their list which are cultural.
☞ Students will create a class definition of culture.

## Time: 1 class period

## Materials:

✄ <u>When the Wind Stops</u> by Charlotte Zolotow
✄ Chalkboard or markerboard

## Procedures:

1. Read <u>When the Wind Stops</u>. Consider this story, and discuss ways in which weather can affect people's lives.

2. Define and discuss culture, as follows: "A system of shared knowledge necessary for surviving as a group and facilitating communication among its members" (Wurzel, 1988, p. 2). Characteristics of culture include communication, language, dress, diet, ways of thinking, attitudes, and celebrations that a group of people share (Wurzel, 1988).

3. Read and discuss this quote with the students: "Perhaps more than any other factor, climate controls culture." (Atwater, M., Baptiste, P., Daniel, L., Hackett, J., Moyer, R., Takemoto, C., & Wilson, N., 1993, p. 66).

4. Discuss all ways weather affects people. Circle the aspects on the class list that pertain to culture.

5. Ask students to redefine culture by creating a class definition, which is understandable at a fourth grade level.

6. Discuss that the class will begin exploring different cultures as they study a meteorology unit.

## Assessment: None

## Homework: None

# LESSON TWO

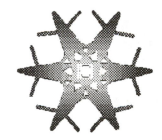

# FORECASTING THE WEATHER

## Objectives:

☛ Students will demonstrate the ability to accurately read the weather report from the newspaper, orally report the daily highs and lows, and orally announce the weather from any country or region of the world. (Adapted from a bulletin board suggestion from "Oceans of Air" T.E., Macmillan/McGraw-Hill, 1993).

☛ Students will interpret the newspaper abbreviations for different weather conditions.

☛ Students will orally compare how weather affected the lives of the people in Cloudy With a Chance of Meatballs with how weather affects their own lives.

☛ Students will achieve scores of 80 percent or higher on a multiple choice/short answer quiz.

## Time: 1 class period

## Materials:

✂ 2"x2" lamine squares for each student in the class
✂ 6-8 overhead markers
✂ A copy of a newspaper weather report for each student
✂ 1 large map of the world on a bulletin board
✂ Cloudy With a Chance of Meatballs by Judi Barrett
✂ Copies of the quiz and answer sheet (included on page 96)

## Procedures:

1. Read Cloudy With a Chance of Meatballs. Discuss how weather affected the lives of the people in this story. Ask the students: How does weather affect our lives? Discuss some of the weather terminology used in the story.

2. Have each student, or groups of two to three students, choose a country (or region of a country), to report on and study for the entire unit. Every student (or group) must chose a different country or region from the list on the board that the teacher has created. This list is created in advance so that resources do not become limited. Also, the list should be comprised of regions that represent all weather conditions the teacher may wish to study.

3. As a class, find a global weather report in the newspaper that lists the major cities of the world. Read together and discuss any weather abbreviations.

4. For practice, by groups or in pairs, have students use the newspaper to ask others at their table to find a particular country's weather.

5. Using the global weather report selected by the class, administer the quiz at this time or the following day.

6. Have a student, or students, demonstrate the daily homework routine of placing his/her updated weather report on the bulletin board. The student writes the weather information on a lamine square with a marker and pins the square to the appropriate country or region on the world map bulletin board.

## Assessment:

Using the multiple choice and short answer quiz on page 96 as a model, have the students use the newspaper to find the highs and lows, and the general weather for the countries or cities listed. The teacher should make up her own quiz using the information from an actual newspaper weather report for authenticity.

*Note:* For global reports, most newspapers print the actual weather of the day before rather than a forecast.

## Homework:

Using the newspaper, each student should find the highs and lows and the general weather that his/her country or region experienced the previous day. In class the following morning, students copy the information onto a lamine square with an overhead marking pen. Every day each student pins the weather information square onto the bulletin board near his/her region or country.

Also, have students conduct a "weather watch" in the newspaper, internet, T.V., and so on for special weather conditions to report to the class if and when they occur.

*Note:* Detailed global weather reports can be found on the internet. Parental permission for a student to "surf the net" for this information is advisable. Have students bring a note from home if your classroom is on-line. Or the teacher can send the internet weather access address in the district mail to the parent for home use.

Name: _____    Date: _____

# Weather Forecast and Report Quiz

On the line, write the letter of the best answer.

____ 1. What is the abbreviation for cloudy?    **a)** Su    **b)** Cy    **c)** CD    **d)** F

____ 2. Which city experienced cloudy weather on Saturday?

   **a)** Caracas    **b)** Cancun    **c)** Geneva    **d)** Toronto

____ 3. The "Lo" means

   a) the lowest temperature the region has ever experienced.
   b) the lowest temperature the region experienced on that day.
   c) the temperature the region was for most of the day.
   d) the lowest temperature a region usually experiences at that time of year.

____ 4. The Lo / Hi under the heading "Normal" refers to

   a) the lows and highs of the day.
   b) the lows and highs of the week.
   c) the usual temperatures for this region on this date.
   d) the average temperatures for the world on that day.

Using the copy of the weather report attached to this quiz, write the answer to each question on the line.

5. What was the high and low temperature for Calgary on Saturday? _____

6. Was the sky sunny or partly cloudy in Calgary on Saturday? _____

7. Name a city that experienced clear skies on Saturday. _____

8. Name a city that experienced a high of 88 on Saturday . _____

9. Was the high for Guadalajara on Saturday higher or lower than the normal

   temperature for that city on this date?_____

10. Find the weather for Acapulco on Saturday. Name an activity you could do in

   that kind of weather.

# LESSON THREE

# HUICHOL INDIAN CULTURE

## Objectives:

☛ Students will define a myth as a literary form.

☛ Students will appreciate a Huichol Legend, and examine some aspects of the diet, lifestyle, and geography of this group of people.

☛ Students will read about the ceremony that Huichol Shamans recited annually at their Harvest Festival of the New Corn and Squash.

☛ Students will list the ways in which weather influenced the Huichol Culture.

☛ Students will evaluate how the lifestyle and diet of the Huichol Indians related to their climate.

## Time: 2 class periods

## Materials:

✄ The Tree That Rains:  The Flood Myth of the Huichol Indians of Mexico by Emery Bernhard

✄ A collection of legends from many other cultures illustrating the ways in which climate influences the people's lives

✄ Overhead projector

✄ Transparencies

✄ Journals for each student for the unit

## Procedures:

1. Read The Tree That Rains: The Flood Myth of the Huichol Indians of Mexico. Discuss why the legend states that the storm came to Watakame's farm (because the people forgot the gods).

2. In cooperative groups, discuss how the storm and floods influenced the diet and settlement of the Huichol people.

3. In group discussions, students evaluate how aspects of Huichol culture complement the climate.

4. On the overhead, place a copy of the author's note page from the back of the book. Students can read about the Harvest Festival of the New Corn and Squash that the people still celebrate today.

5. Pass out legends from many different cultures. Students may read and share these legends. With a friend, have students discuss how weather influenced the culture as told by other legends from around world.

6. Pass out a journal to each student. Explain that this journal will be used periodically throughout the unit. Today's prompt: How might your culture be different if you lived where the Huichol Indians live?

7. Change daily weather bulletin board reports.

## Assessment:

The journal will be graded at the end of the unit using a checklist which indicates whether or not the student responded to the prompt on each entry. A copy of this checklist is included on this page and on page 213 of the Assessment Appendix.

## Homework:

Record daily weather report for country or region.

## Checklist for Journal Responses

Student Name:

| Lesson number | Prompt | Did respond | Did not respond |
|---|---|---|---|
| Three | Huichol Indians | | |
| Six | Tornado fears | | |
| Seven | Origin legend | | |
| Eight | Hurricane, monsoon or typhoon? | | |
| Nine | Water list | | |
| Thirteen | Lowering $CO_2$ emissions | | |

Copyright © 1998 by Allyn and Bacon

# LESSON FOUR

# WEATHER RESEARCH

## Objectives:

☛ Students will recall weather phenomena with which they are familiar.
☛ Students will define "weather" and "climate," and compare how these words are related.
☛ Students will demonstrate the ability to gather weather information from encyclopedias and world almanacs.

## Time: 1 class period

## Materials:

✄ Markerboard or chalkboard
✄ Encyclopedias for each country chosen
✄ World almanacs
✄ Trade books with weather information
✄ Copies of student text, "Oceans of Air," or any student meteorology text
✄ <u>Weather</u> by Howard E. Smith

## Procedures:

1. Read <u>Weather</u> by Howard E. Smith. Discuss the distinction that the book makes between weather and climate.

2. List on the board the various weather conditions with which the students are familiar. Do not erase the list.

3. Distribute reference books. Have the students identify the weather or climate section for their country or region and list the common types of weather experienced there.

4. Student or groups of students then write their names on the board list next to the type(s) of weather that their country or region experiences. Each student, or group, will become an expert in one of these areas.

5. Change daily weather bulletin board.

## Assessment: None.

## Homework:

Record daily weather report for country or region.

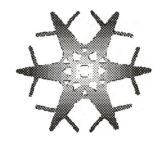

# LESSON FIVE

# EXPERT REPORTS

## Objectives:

☛ Students will compile and organize weather-related information from encyclopedias and/or trade books.

☛ Students will compose a factual report from their notes on weather.

## Time: 3 class periods

## Materials:

✂ Encyclopedias, trade books, and other reference materials
✂ Paper
✂ Storms by Seymour Simon

## Procedures:

1. Before the lesson, the teacher must consider the types of weather each country or region experiences. Then the teacher should assign "expert reports" on these same weather conditions. In this way, the teacher can ensure that "expert reports" will be given on all of the weather conditions to be studied.

2. Read Storms to capture student interest.

3. Assign the weather condition for which each student, or group, will become expert. "Expert reports" should be in paragraph form and presented orally.

4. Pass out reference materials and have the students begin their research. Reports should include, but not be limited by the following criteria: where the weather condition occurs, why it occurs, its capability for damaging an area, and a general description of the weather.

5. At the close of each day, discuss any problems the students are having and change daily weather bulletin board.

## Assessment:

Expert written and oral reports are graded with rubrics included in the Assessment Appendix on pages 210 and 211.

## Homework:

Record daily weather report for country or region.

# LESSON SIX

# TORNADO!

## Objectives:

☛ Students will identify with the fear that storms and bad weather can bring to themselves and others.

☛ Students will recall why being treated differently would be more frightening to a person with special needs than an approaching tornado.

☛ Students who became experts on tornadoes will present their reports to the class.

☛ Students will analyze what new information should be added to the existing report and include it.

☛ Students will construct a replica of a tornado.

**Time:** 2 class periods

## Materials:

✂ Overhead projector

✂ Directions for constructing a tornado in a bottle (included on page 102)

✂ 72-liter bottles (enough for each group of four students)

✂ Illustrations of tornadoes

✂ The Storm by Marc Harshman

✂ Markerboard or chalkboard

✂ "Windows On Science" laser disc from Earth Science, Volume 2

✂ Copies of "expert reports" about tornadoes (one for each student)

## Procedures:

1. Students present their "expert reports" on tornadoes and distribute copies.

2. Show "Windows on Science" laser disc. As students watch this disc, they will have their copy of the tornado report in front of them. As they listen to the disc, they should note new information on the report to be rewritten as homework.

3. Form groups of four students to replicate a tornado in a soda bottle, following the directions on page 102.

4. Read The Storm. Discuss the child's fears about being stuck in a wheelchair. He wants his classmates to stop thinking he is more afraid than they are because of his physical condition. He has more fears related to being singled out than about the approaching tornado.

5. Ask students to discuss the fears of the boy in the story.  If they were in a wheelchair, what do they think their biggest fear would be?  Ask students to substantiate the boy's feelings.  Discuss other ways people with physical handicaps are labeled or judged by non-handicapped people.  Is it fair to assume some people have more limits and fears than others because of their physical condition?

6. Have students respond in their journals after this discussion.  Prompt:  What fears might you have if you were caught in a tornado?  Share ideas.  Remind tomorrow's group that they need to be ready to share thunderstorm/snowstorm reports.

7. Change daily weather bulletin board.

## Assessment:

Written and oral presentations of the tornado reports will be assessed using the rubrics included in the Assessment Appendix on pages 210 and 211.

## Homework:

Record daily weather report for country or region.  Rewrite tornado report with new information gleaned from the laser disc presentation.

---

# Directions For Creating A Tornado

1. Purchase "The Tornado Tube," a small cylinder-shaped piece of plastic sold at most teaching supply stores.

2. Clean two plastic soda bottles (must be of the same size).

3. Fill one bottle half-way with water.

4. Screw "The Tornado Tube" onto the mouth of the bottle.

5. Turn second soda bottle upside down and twist it onto the top of "The Tornado Tube."

6. When the bottles are tightly connected, vigorously swirl the tube in circles in an upright position (like a baton) for thirty seconds to one minute.

7. Quickly upend the tube so that the empty bottle is on the bottom.  As the water begins to move into the lower bottle, a tornado will appear in the center of the water.

---

# LESSON SEVEN

# SNOW AND THUNDER STORMS

## Objectives:

☛ Students will read Nandi, West African, and Chactaw legends about thunder and lightning.
☛ Students will compare and contrast the legends' explanations.
☛ Students will present their expert reports on thunderstorms and snowstorms.
☛ Students will analyze what new information should be added to the existing report and include it.

## Time: 2-3 class periods

## Materials:

✄ "Windows on Science" laser disc. Earth Science, Volume 2
✄ Bringing The Rain To Kapiti Plain by Verna Aardema
✄ The Story Of Lightning And Thunder by Ashley Bryan
✄ How Thunder and Lightning Came To Be by Beatrice Orcutt Harrell
✄ Copies of "expert reports" about thunderstorms and snowstorms (one for each student)
✄ Student questionnaire (included on page 104)

## Procedures:

1. Students present their "expert reports" on snowstorms and distribute copies.

2. Show "Windows on Science" laser disc. As students watch this disc, they will have their copy of the snowstorm report in front of them. As they listen to the disc, they should note new information on the report to be rewritten as homework.

3. Students present their "expert reports" on thunderstorms and distribute copies.

4. Show "Windows on Science" laser disc. As students watch this disc, they will have their copy of the thunderstorm report in front of them. As they listen to the disc, they should note new information on the report to be rewritten as homework.

5. Read The Story of Lightning and Thunder, How Thunder and Lightning Came to Be, and Bringing The Rain To Kapiti Plain.

6.  Have the students answer the student questionnaire (included on page 104) individually.  When they are finished, have them compare and share answers in small groups.

7.  In their journals students will write about how thunderstorms influence culture. Prompt:  Create a mini-legend explaining the origins of thunder and lightning from your perspective.  Be creative.

8.  Remind students that the next day's "expert reports" will be on monsoons, typhoons and hurricanes.

9.  Change daily weather bulletin board.

## Assessment:

Written "expert reports" and oral presentations on snowstorms and thunderstorms will be graded using the rubrics included in the Assessment Appendix on pages 210 and 211.

## Homework:

Record daily weather reports for country or region.  Rewrite snowstorm or thunderstorm reports with new information gleaned from the laser disc presentation.

---

## Student Questionnaire

1.  In a sentence or two, summarize how the West African legend explained thunder and lightning.

2.  In a sentence or two, summarize how the Chactaw legend explained thunder and lightning.

3.  In a sentence or two, summarize how the Nandi legend explained thunder and lightning.

4.  Using a three-ring Venn diagram, compare and contrast these three legends.

5.  Can you think of other stories you have read that explain an event or  occurrence from different perspectives?

6.  When have you and your family or friends seen something in different ways? Write a descriptive paragraph about such an occurrence.

---

# LESSON EIGHT

# HURRICANES, MONSOONS, AND TYPHOONS

## Objectives:

☛ Students will read Hurricane.
☛ Students will present their expert reports on hurricanes, monsoons, and typhoons.
☛ Students will analyze what new information should be added to the existing reports and include it.

## Time: 1 class period

## Materials:

✂ Hurricane by David Wiesner
✂ Copies of "expert reports" about hurricanes, monsoons, and typhoons (one for each student)
✂ "Windows on Science" laser disc, Earth Science, Volume 2

## Procedures:

1. Students present their "expert reports" on hurricanes and distribute copies.

2. Students present their "expert reports" on monsoons and distribute copies.

3. Students present their "expert reports" on typhoons and distribute copies.

4. Discuss differences between monsoon, typhoon, and hurricane. Typhoons are hurricanes that develop in the Pacific Ocean. They got their name from the Chinese word meaning "great wind." Monsoons are winds in the Indian Ocean that change direction with the seasons. The name comes from the Arabic Word meaning "season."

5. Show "Windows on Science" laser disc. As students watch this disc, they will have their copies of the "expert reports" in front of them. As they listen to the disc, they should note new information on the report to be rewritten as homework.

6. Read Hurricane. Discuss how hurricanes influenced the people in this story.

7. In their journals students will write about how monsoons, typhoons, and hurricanes influence culture. Prompt: Choose either a hurricane, a

monsoon, or a typhoon.  Explain where they occur, and what effects this weather can have on culture.

8.  Remind students that the next day's "expert reports" will be on droughts.

9.  Change daily weather bulletin board.

## Assessment:

Written "expert reports" and oral presentations on monsoons, typhoons, and hurricanes will be graded using the rubrics included in the Assessment Appendix on pages 210 and 211.

## Homework:

Record daily weather reports for country or region. Rewrite monsoon, typhoon, or hurricane reports with new information gleaned from the laser disc presentation.

# LESSON NINE

# DROUGHTS

## Objectives:

☛ Students will read a Mayan Tale, entitled <u>Rain Player</u>.
☛ Students will present their expert reports on droughts.

## Time: 1 class period

## Materials:

✀ <u>Rain Player</u> by David Wisniewski
✀ Copies of "expert reports" about droughts (one for each student)

## Procedures:

1. Students present their "expert reports" on droughts and distribute copies.

2. Read the <u>Rain Player</u>. Discuss how droughts influenced the people and their culture in this story.

3. In their journals students will write about how droughts influence culture. Prompt: List ten things you do in your life that require water. Choose some of these and discuss how you might do these things differently if you lived in an area that had severe droughts and had no way to purchase water from outside sources. Share ideas orally.

4. Change daily weather bulletin board.

## Assessment:

Written "expert reports" and oral presentations on droughts will be graded using the rubrics included in the Assessment Appendix on pages 210 and 211.

## Homework:

Record daily weather report for country or region.

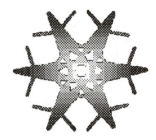

# LESSON TEN

# INUIT CULTURE

## Objectives:

☞ Students will read an Inuit Story entitled <u>Houses of Snow, Skin and Bones</u>.
☞ Students will discuss how closely their lifestyle is tied to their climate.
☞ Students will defend a thesis statement.

## Time: 1 class period

## Materials:

✄ Markerboard or chalkboard
✄ <u>Houses of Snow, Skin and Bones</u> by Bonnie Shemie

## Procedures:

1. Read <u>Houses of Snow, Skin and Bones</u>. Discuss how weather and/or climate affects the Inuit life.

2. In a paragraph, have the students evaluate and justify the following statement: "The aspects of Inuit culture discussed in this story are necessary for the survival of the people."

3. When paragraphs are complete, students share responses and compare ideas.

4. Change daily weather bulletin board.

## Assessment: None.

## Homework:

Record daily weather report for country or region.

# LESSON ELEVEN

# CULTURE VS. CLIMATE

## Objectives:

☛ Students will investigate the influence of weather upon one or two cultural aspects of the country or region they are researching.

☛ Students will orally present their findings.

☛ Students will analyze characteristics which are a part of the students' culture.

## Time: 3 class periods

## Materials:

✂ Markerboard or chalkboard

✂ Butcher paper for process grid, divided into 5 columns and 5 rows

✂ Reference materials on students' countries or regions

## Procedures:

1. Have students refer to the definitions of culture generated at the beginning of the unit and list as many aspects of culture as possible. Then have the students indicate which ones are influenced by weather or climate.

2. Using reference materials, students investigate the details of the culture/climate relationship for the particular country or region that they are studying and present their findings to the class.

3. When all presentations are made, uncover the butcher paper process grid, fill in the chart as a whole class, and compare and contrast cultural responses to climate.

4. Make a list of any aspects of culture which are also a cultural trait in the students' lives. Discuss other characteristics of the students' cultures that originated in other regions of the world.

5. Change daily bulletin board.

## Assessment:

The rating scale for the cultural presentation is included in the Assessment Appendix on page 212.

## Homework:

Record daily weather report for country or region.

# LESSON TWELVE

# OZONE DEPLETION

## Objectives:

☞ Students will recall that ozone is a factor that affects the amount of ultraviolet rays that enter the earth's atmosphere.
☞ Students will identify the relationship between ozone depletion and skin cancer.
☞ Students will list causes of ozone depletion, and circle causes for which personal responsibility can be taken.
☞ Students will pledge to do their part to protect the ozone layer.

## Time: 2 class periods

## Materials:

✄ Background information on ozone depletion (included on page 111)
✄ Globe, or large map of the world

## Procedures:

1. Pass out the background information on ozone depletion (included on page 111) and have the students read it silently. As a whole class or in small groups, list some of the causes of ozone depletion and its negative effects on many parts of the world.

2. Discuss personal responsibility for the environment. As a whole class or in small groups, return to the list of causes to circle those aspects for which it is possible to take personal responsibility.

3. Give students an opportunity to pledge to be environmentally responsible for the preservation of the ozone layer. Perhaps the class can adopt an environmental project for the rest of the year. If your school is connected to the internet, students can e-mail students at schools around the world to share ideas about ozone depletion and environmental protection. Many schools have e-mail addresses, and there are internet programs which connect schools for the purpose of discussing environmental issues.

4. Change daily bulletin board.

## Assessment: None.

## Homework:

Record daily weather for country or region.

# Ozone Depletion

Ozone is a form of oxygen that is mostly found in the layer of our atmosphere called the *stratosphere*. This ozone layer is responsible for keeping out most of the sun's ultraviolet rays, which are harmful to humans. Scientists have found "holes" in the ozone layer over the continent of Antarctica. They are not big holes, actually they are more like extreme thinning of the ozone layer in this area. These "holes" are significantly affecting many countries on the southern hemisphere, such as New Zealand, Australia, and the southern tip of South America. As a result of these holes, and the overall thinning of the ozone layer over other continents as well, increased amounts of ultraviolet rays from the sun are entering our atmosphere. These ultraviolet rays are causing increased amounts of skin cancer. While countries nearest the poles are experiencing the most complications right now, ozone depletion is occurring all over the world, and affecting all people. It is a global concern.

There are many factors that contribute to ozone depletion. Some factors are natural, such as geography, temperature, light, and wind. And there really isn't anything people can do about this. However, there are many other contributing factors to ozone depletion that we can prevent. Scientists have found that a major factor in ozone depletion is chlorofluorocarbons (CFC's). These are chemicals found in refrigerator coolants, many spray bottles, and air conditioning units for homes and cars. CFC's are also used in the manufacturing of styrofoam products and some furniture. While CFC's are the main contributors to ozone depletion, some other human activities play a small role in ozone depletion as well. These include deforestation, and burning of fossil fuels.

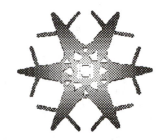

# LESSON THIRTEEN

# GLOBAL WARMING

## Objectives:

☛ Students will define global warming.
☛ Students will recall that carbon dioxide ($CO_2$) affects the earth's temperatures.
☛ Students will list objects that emit carbon dioxide.
☛ Students will list activities that prevent excessive carbon dioxide levels from entering our atmosphere.
☛ Students will cite which countries have influenced global warming.
☛ Students will determine what lifestyle changes could reverse this trend.

## Time: 2 class periods

## Materials:

✄ Background information on global warming (included on page 113)
✄ Markerboard or chalkboard

## Procedures:

1. Pass out the fact sheet on global warming (included on page 113) and have the students read it silently.  As a whole class or in small groups, define global warming and list some of the causes.  Have the students orally summarize the relationship between $CO_2$ and the earth's temperature.

2.  Review the discussion of personal responsibility for the environment.  As a whole class or in small groups, list objects that emit $CO_2$ as well as activities which prevent excessive $CO_2$ levels from entering the atmosphere.

3. Students will consider which countries help create extra carbon dioxide.  They will realize that it is a global problem.

4. Students will respond to this prompt in their journal.  "What can you and your family do to personally lower carbon dioxide emissions in the atmosphere?"

5. Change daily bulletin board.

## Assessment: None.

## Homework:

Record daily weather report for country or region.

# GLOBAL WARMING

Gasses in our atmosphere trap some of the solar energy that reaches earth. We call this process the *greenhouse effect* because the gasses work like a greenhouse by trapping heat. In a good way, the greenhouse effect helps to keep our earth warm. However, when levels of certain gasses in the atmosphere increase, as many scientists believe, then the atmosphere traps even more heat. This causes the earth to get warmer. An overall increase in the earth's temperatures is called *global warming*. Many scientists are worried that the greenhouse effect is increasing now, and that global warming may lead to changes in climate all over the world.

There are many factors that can cause global warming. Burning fossil fuels such as coal, oil, and natural gas releases large amounts of gasses into the air. These gasses trap heat. Gasses such as carbon dioxide, methane and nitrous oxide, as well as some chemicals such as chlorofluorocarbons (CFC's), can be called *greenhouse gasses* because of their heat-trapping characteristics. In some ways, the amounts of these gasses in our atmosphere can be controlled by people. For example, there is an increase in carbon dioxide in the atmosphere from using gas-powered transportation such as cars and airplanes. Also, a decrease in green plants and vegetation on earth (deforestation) can increase global warming because green plants consume carbon dioxide and create oxygen. A method of clearing land for farming called "slash and burn" can also reduce vegetation. Though we will discuss deforestation in more detail in lesson fourteen, these land-clearing techniques contribute to global warming.

Copyright © 1998 Allyn and Bacon

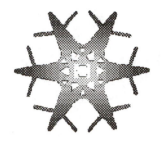

# LESSON FOURTEEN

# DEFORESTATION

## Objectives:

☛ Students will locate the major rain forests, using a large map of the world.

☛ Students will role-play to gain multiple perspectives on the problems of and proposed solutions to deforestation.

## Time: 2 class periods

## Materials:

✄ Pictures of rain forests (easily available in environmental magazines)

✄ Background information on deforestation (included on page 115)

✄ Copies of a map of the world

✄ Role play scenarios (included on pages 116 and 117) copied onto 5" x 7" index cards

## Procedures:

1. Share pictures of rain forests with students.

2. Pass out a copy of a world map to every student. Using an encyclopedia, look up "tropical rain forests." (Most have good maps of the world with the forests' exact locations.) Have students color or shade the areas of the world where rain forests are found.

3. Read deforestation background information with students (included on page 115).

4. Pass out role-playing cards to each student. Tell students that they should read about their character sketch, and write some ideas about what their character might say if they were confronted about the problem of rain forest destruction and its preservation.

5. In groups, have students share their characters' feelings and beliefs about humankind's use and abuse of the rain forests. Have students make an outline of the discussion.

6. The next day, ask students to exchange their character for a different character. Again, have them write some ideas about their characters' feelings about deforestation, and present their viewpoint to others in a group. Again, have students make an outline of the discussion.

7. As a class, share ideas that made one another appreciate a new perspective.

8. As with ozone depletion, if you have internet access, have students e-mail other people for their opinions regarding deforestation and global warming, and how they are affecting their lives.

9. Change daily bulletin board.

## Assessment:

Informal observation and anecdotal records work nicely for this exercise. It takes at least 15-20 minutes for a group to debate this issue from multiple perspectives. After two or more group discussions, it is possible to listen to every student.

In addition to anecdotal records, students turn in an outline of what they expressed in group discussion. This outline is graded on a rating scale which is included in the Assessment Appendix on page 213.

## Homework:

Record daily weather report for country or region.

### Deforestation

Forests, especially rain forests, create much of our earth's oxygen supply. It creates this oxygen and absorbs carbon dioxide. The rain forests absorb more carbon dioxide than any other element on earth. This absorption of carbon dioxide helps reduce global warming because carbon dioxide helps to make the atmosphere warmer. However, our rain forests are being destroyed at an alarming rate. If we don't do something to protect them, many scientists think all of our rain forests will soon be completely gone.

There are many reasons for the deterioration of the rain forests. In many of the countries where rain forests are found, human population is increasing and the growth of cities spreads into the rain forest areas. Also, there are many valuable resources in the rain forests. An example of a valuable resource found in the rain forests is mahogany wood, which is used for building furniture. Logging companies cut this and other rain forest wood in large quantities, and sell it to countries all over the world. Another valuable resource are rain forest plants. From them medicine is made that assists in the treatment of cancer and other diseases. Additionally, farmers can also damage the rain forests. They often use a method of farming called "slash and burn" which is harmful to the rain forests. In this method, the farmer slashes an area of land, lets the vegetation die and become brittle, and burns the area for farmland. Many farmers and large companies also use the slash and burn method to clear land for raising cattle. As the world population is increasing, cattle are needed for meat production.

# Role-Playing Scenarios

Copyright © 1998 by Allyn and Bacon

You are a farmer of the rain forests in Thailand and part of a cultural group called the "Lua." You practice slash and burn, but are not responsible for destroying rain forests.  You need to continue slash and burn, because it is an effective way for your family to survive. You don't understand the scientific term "global warming." Your people have been farming this way for centuries.

You are a native to the rain forests of Central America. You are a Mayan farmer and your family has always lived in the rain forest. You do not destroy it, you live in harmony with it. You have always made your living growing crops. With all the land development, the cities are starting to move in where you live. You worry that you and your family will be homeless.

You are a scientist from an international company that cuts down trees from the rain forests.  Many of these plants and trees contain materials that you can use to make medicines to fight cancer and other diseases.   You do not want to support deforestation because it causes environmental problems, However, you tell yourself that saving peoples' lives is a more important issue.

You are an environmentalist from Canada and worried about the rain forests. You know that deforestation is creating global problems, including global warming and ozone depletion. Your country is seeing higher rates of skin cancer due to ozone depletion as it is a country near the North pole.  Preserving the rain forests will help preserve ozone.  It is your number one priority.

You are a land developer who is clearing rain forests to create space for housing. You are sorry that the rain forests are being destroyed, but you feel it is more important for people to have jobs and places to live. As the world's population continues to grow, people have to live somewhere.

You are a member of a global environmental group whose purpose is to unite globally to preserve the rain forests. You know that our rain forests can help reduce global warming, and indirectly reduce ozone depletion. You represent many different nations in your fight to get countries and private businesses to be more environmentally responsible.

You are living in Australia. You have frequent skin cancer problems, which your doctor believes is a result of ozone depletion. If the rain forests keep being destroyed, more $CO_2$ will remain in the air where you live because there will be fewer trees to absorb it. You will continue to have medical problems. You don't care what the world has to do to stop deforestation. You think preserving the rain forests is the first priority.

You are a cattle rancher who uses slash and burn practices to clear land for raising cattle. This is your job. It is how you support your family. Raising cattle helps to feed people all over the world. Many countries buy your meat. If you didn't raise cattle, many people wouldn't have enough food to eat, including your family.

# LESSON FIFTEEN

# FINAL ASSESSMENT

## Objectives:

☛ Students will take an exam which measures knowledge, reasoning skills, and feelings about culture, meteorology, and global environmental issues.

☛ Students will evaluate the structure of the unit, lesson plans, interest in the topic.

## Time: 1 class period

## Materials:

✄ End of unit test (included in the Assessment Appendix on page 214)

✄ Student evaluation of the meteorology unit (included in the Assessment Appendix on page 215)

## Procedures:

1. Administer end of unit test.

2. Administer unit evaluation.

3. Turn in journals.

## Assessment:

End of unit test will be graded. As answers will vary according to implementation of unit, an answer sheet is not included. Journal will be graded (rating scale is included on page 98 and in the Assessment Appendix on page 213). Student evaluation of the meteorology unit will be used to assist the teacher in altering the unit for next year.

## Homework: None.

# Summary and suggestions

My school is in a middle-to upper-income area of Southern Orange County. My class is comprised of 27 fourth grade students, with 15 girls and 12 boys. The parents are extremely supportive of in-class and out-of-class work. In the classroom, they are very active as well, volunteering weekly. I usually have 1-2 parents a day assisting in the classroom in any way that benefits the students. However, these parents do prefer that subjects are taught traditionally, and they are not familiar, overall, with multicultural education.

I implemented this multicultural meteorology unit in September of 1995. I intended this unit as a solid introduction to multicultural education and as a preparation for later units that would delve more deeply into cultural issues and multiple perspectives. Through student feedback, student evaluations, and teacher observation, I am satisfied that this unit accomplished its goals.

Throughout the year, we studied historical events such as the building of the transcontinental railroad, the philosophy of Manifest Destiny, and other issues that affected specific ethnic groups in America. At the time, it appeared quite easy and natural for the students to employ the skills necessary to consider these events and philosophies from many different cultural perspectives. On an individual basis, many students even pointed out injustices, stereotypes, and alternative viewpoints on issues before I formally discussed the issues with the class. I was quite proud of how well they were able to consider differing points of view.

I think this meteorology unit set the tone for the year and began the class thinking from different perspectives from the first week of school. In addition to the unit being successful from an academic standpoint, the students' verbal responses and the student evaluation forms indicated that they really enjoyed the unit. Specifically, they enjoyed being responsible for teaching the rest of the class about a particular weather condition, and the cultural aspects tied to weather from the country or region they chose to study. This was not a total surprise as the idea of "expert groups" has, in my experience, always proved to be a successful strategy in the upper grades.

In the spirit of this enthusiasm, many students shared this unit with their parents. While most parents were pleased with the unit, a few parents raised concerns. The most common concern was that I was using a supplement to the district's physical science unit. Another concern was that in lesson fourteen, some students, through role-play, were asked to take the position of someone who puts their own interests above that of saving the rain forests. One of my parents expressed the opinion that it was "environmentally irresponsible" to promote any other view besides preservation. I also had two parents concerned that I had encouraged the use of the internet in lessons twelve and thirteen. It placed too many time constraints on them because they needed to chaperone their children on the internet.

In response to the three parental concerns, I did make adjustments to some aspects of the unit. I used more lessons from the Macmillan/McGraw-Hill series than I had originally intended, so as to assure parents that I was definitely incorporating large portions of the district's textbook. This resulted in a longer meteorology unit than I had anticipated.   Also, in lesson twelve, after the few complaints, I did not encourage using the internet access for lesson thirteen. While I think the internet can be a valuable tool, I agreed that it was not fair to place time demands on the parents.  Next year this will not be an issue, as our school will have internet access. I will not make it a home project.

On a positive note, I was equally surprised by how well the students responded to the role-playing exercise in lesson fourteen.  They asked me to prepare a similar exercise for every unit of study. (This kept me quite busy researching information to create characters!) We made debates a part of every unit.  It became the highlight of the year, something students looked forward to at the close of every unit.  I think they really enjoyed the freedom that tends to result from studying issues from many viewpoints.   Students began to feel confident that their ideas weren't necessarily wrong just because they weren't "in the book," or straight from my mouth.  It is also a great relief when students realize that more than one answer is acceptable if it can be justified.

## Personal Profile

I have been teaching elementary school in Southern California for 7 years.  During this time, I have taught grades 3, 4, and kindergarten.  Like most teachers, I have taught many kinds of learners, ranging from Gifted Students to Special Needs to students learning English as a second language.  During my first year of teaching, I discovered that one thing all of my students shared was a love of science.  This enthusiasm for experimenting and inquiring directed me to become involved in several science organizations and clubs for teachers.  I also took a few extra college classes in Earth Science and Chemistry so that I would have an adequate background to handle their curiosity, and endless questions. During this process, I have come to love science as my students do.

In addition to my interest in Science, in 1996 I completed my masters' degree in Multicultural Education.  This degree has been a great asset in assisting me to find ways for all of my students to become excited about their education. This degree was also the inspiration for this multicultural meteorology unit.

# CHAPTER SIX

# We, the people...but which people?
# A study of America's primary documents
## by Barbara Hamm

In California, where I teach, an important section of the fifth grade Social Studies curriculum is the introduction of the Declaration of Independence, the Constitution, and the Bill of Rights as documents which set forth the freedoms which we enjoy as Americans today. Students growing up in past years have studied this period of history as one in which all Americans were considered to be "created equal," and where justice was established for everyone.

However, as revisionist thinking has shown to bear, equality for each person regardless of gender or ethnicity was clearly not the case. According to Howard Zinn, in A People's History of the United States, "Some Americans were clearly omitted from the circle of united interest drawn by the Declaration of Independence: Indians, blacks, slaves, women" (p. 72).

There is a need for teacher and student materials which present America's primary documents within the thinking and the philosophy of the times in which they were written, and truthfully represent the facts of just who was afforded rights by the new government, and who wasn't.

After searching my school library, public library, and the local teacher supply store, the only booklet I found was Voices in African American History: The American Revolution, which discusses the effects on African Americans of the Declaration of Independence and the Constitution. Because I could find so little to help me teach my students about the inequalities of our country's founding documents, I developed my own materials.

The following interdisciplinary instructional unit offers eight lessons, which can be used in combination with an existing United States history curriculum and adapted as needed to fit any upper grade elementary classroom. A mixture of social studies, language arts, art, music, and mathematics make up the unit. The entire unit covers thirteen to seventeen class periods, depending on the amount of time a teacher may wish to spend on an individual lesson plan. The unit is flexible, however, and may be shortened if the teacher uses all the lessons together or selects only a few.

Integrated throughout the unit is a multicultural and human relations approach to the study of the Declaration of Independence, the Constitution, and the Bill of Rights, with the hope that many of the concepts brought up in the lessons can be applied to present-day situations, as well.

# Quick View Chart of the Instructional Unit

| Lesson One<br>"What do we already know?" | Lesson Two<br>"Letters, we get letters..." |
|---|---|
| Students use an inquiry chart and a true/false tool to assess their prior knowledge of the material to be presented in the unit. | Students study the grievances presented in the Declaration of Independence, and compose a letter to Thomas Jefferson from the perspective of a woman, a Native American, or an African American, expressing their grievances regarding the document. |
| Lesson Three<br>"Presenting Our Preamble" | Lesson Four<br>"Inherit the Wind" |
| After studying the preamble to the Constitution, students create a class preamble which applies to all students and incorporates an appreciation for acceptance and diversity. | After studying and analyzing the Bill of Rights, students write their own, citing individual rights they feel each citizen should have. Students then create a document which displays the rights they have expressed. |
| Lesson Five<br>"The Haves vs. the Have Nots" | Lesson Six<br>"Tuneful biographies" |
| A game for two teams involving math skills introduces interesting facts and figures from this period of history. | Students research a famous woman, Native American or African American of this time, and then write a song about him/her to the tune of "Yankee Doodle." |
| Lesson Seven<br>"Great Gazettes" | Lesson Eight<br>"In Their Shoes" |
| Students use the "Five W's" of good reporting to create a gazette of the late 18th century. | Students use a variety of suggested methods to simulate situations and problems encountered by women, African Americans, and Native Americans in the late 18th century. |

# LESSON ONE

# WHAT DO WE ALREADY KNOW?

## Objectives:

☛ Students list their prior knowledge of the roles of women, African Americans, and Native Americans at the time of the Constitution.
☛ Students apply their existing knowledge to the completion of a true/false tool.
☛ Students discuss the results of the true/false tool.

## Time: One class period

## Materials:

✂ Butcher paper for inquiry chart
✂ Handout for each student: "What Do We Already Know?  A True/False Quiz"
✂ Answer key (Handout and Answer Key are included on pages 124, 125, and 126).

## Procedures:

1. On a sheet of butcher paper attached to the wall, the teacher draws three columns entitled: "What We Already Know," "What We Want to Know," and "How Will We Find Out?"  The teacher then asks the class what they already know about the roles of women, African Americans, and Native Americans during the end of the 18th century.  The chart is completed by asking the students what they might want to learn, and how they plan to learn about it.

2. Administer the true/false tool and give the class enough time to complete it. Distribute a copy of the answers to each student, review each item, and encourage discussion.  Most likely, students will be surprised by the answers.

3.  Have the students start a "We the People...But Which People?" folder. The true/false tool and the answer key are inserted as the first two pages.  Refer to them when necessary to reinforce concepts being learned.

## Assessment:

Students may not have a great deal of accurate information to bring to the inquiry chart or the true/false tool.  Assure them that these are not graded.

The teacher may use the  "Classroom Discussion Scoresheet" (included in the Assessment Appendix on  page 216) to evaluate the discussion.

## Why This Lesson?

This lesson allows the teacher to review what the students have already learned about these three groups of people in American history and to present new knowledge in a fun, non-threatening way.  The true/false tool should lead to a good amount of discussion, and serve as a springboard for further activities in this unit.

# What Do We Already Know?
## A True/False Quiz

Please circle true  (T) or false (F) to answer the following questions:

T   F   1. Abigail Adams, wife of John Adams, was one of the first to push for women's' rights in American history.

T   F   2. Thomas Jefferson, the chief author of the Declaration of Independence, hated slavery and refused to own any slaves.

T   F   3. George Washington was one of the three largest slaveowners in the South.

T   F   4. One of the most respected poets of the late 18th century was a black woman.

T   F   5. The original version of the Declaration of Independence held King George III of England responsible for the slave trade.

T   F   6. According to the Constitution, freed African slaves could vote.

T   F   7. According to the Constitution, women could vote as long as they were married.

T   F   8. No women voted in the first presidential election of 1789.

T   F   9. One of the requirements to vote as set forth in the Constitution was that the individual be a land owner.

T   F   10. All thirteen states ratified (approved) the Constitution right away, because they were all so eager to have it take effect.

T   F   11. Vermont was the first state to abolish slavery.

T   F   12. The word "slavery" is mentioned 7 times in the Constitution.

T   F   13. No slaves ever returned to Africa.

T   F   14. Out of the total population of the colonies in 1800, only 1 percent were of African origin.

T   F   15. Native Americans were not allowed to fight on either side during the Revolutionary War.

T   F   16. African slaves volunteered to fight in the Revolutionary War, in the hopes that they might be freed afterwards.

T   F   17. Many signers of the Declaration of Independence and the Constitution were major army and naval heroes of the Revolutionary War.

T   F   18. No women chose to be on the battlefield during the Revolutionary War.

T   F   19. Even though men were off fighting during the Revolutionary War, their wives were still not allowed to handle money or have anything to do with the family businesses.

T   F   20. The Constitution says that if a slave runs away to a state that does not have slavery, he or she is automatically free.

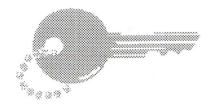

# Answer Key
# for
# "What Do We Already Know?"

1. **True**    Abigail Adams strongly believed in equality for women; she spoke and wrote on feminist issues before and after her husband became the second president of the United States.

2. **False**    Although Thomas Jefferson had a lot of misgivings about slavery, he owned more than 200 slaves, and was reluctant to abolish that institution.

3. **True**    George Washington owned many slaves who worked, lived at, and maintained his huge plantation at Mount Vernon, Virginia.

4. **True**    Phillis Wheatley, a slave most of her life, learned to read and write while employed by her owner. Her poetry was so popular that she even traveled to England to meet the king.

5. **True**    Along with blaming King George for everything else, the authors of the Declaration also threw in the slave trade, hoping that it would relieve them of some of the guilt and negative aspects associated with this institution. This section of grievances was thrown out before the document was finalized.

6. **False**    According to the Constitution, no African Americans could vote, whether freed or enslaved.

7. **False**    According to the Constitution, no women were allowed to vote, whether married or single.

8. **False**    Because of a "mistake" in the New Jersey State Constitution, women were allowed the vote in this election, and many took advantage of this opportunity. When the legislators (all men), realized what had occurred, they quickly changed the law so that only men could vote.

9. **True**    In order to vote in the United States, a person had to be male and a property owner. This virtually eliminated all Africans, Native Americans, and women at that time in history.

10. **False**    According to the rules for ratification of the Constitution, it only had to be approved by 9 of the 13 states before it went into effect.

11. True    In July of 1777, Vermont became the first state to officially abolish slavery. It was soon followed by other New England and Middle Atlantic states.

12. False   The word "slavery" is not mentioned at all in the entire Constitution. Instead, the document talks about "persons held to service or labor."

13. False   In 1792, about 1,200 African Americans who fought for the British in the Revolutionary War were offered transportation and 20 acres of land in Sierra Leone on the west coast of Africa. Other African Americans who had fought for the British went to Canada, England, and the West Indies. A total of 14,000 left the United States, freed from their slavery by the British.

14. False   Out of the total population ( 3 million) of the colonies at that time, half were women, and 20 percent were African American.  Eighty percent of these Africans were slaves.

15. False   Native Americans fought on both sides during the Revolutionary War. The Patriots took revenge on those who fought on the British side by burning their villages and setting fire to their fields. They rewarded those who fought on their side by pushing them further westward and taking their land.

16. True    The colonists were hesitant to employ African slaves in the army for fear that they would run away. However, the British offered instant freedom to any African American who would fight on their side, and many enlisted to go to war for King George. The Patriots did eventually recruit African soldiers, but after the war, the slaves were sent back to their masters and they realized that little had changed.

17. False   Although a handful actually fought in the war, most were wealthy landowners who paid poor whites and even their African slaves to fight in their place.

18. False   Women were discouraged from fighting in the war, but several went to the battlefields anyway to bring water, food, and support to the soldiers. Some even dressed as men and fought alongside the male soldiers at important battles.

19. True    While their husbands were away at war, many women were forced to make important financial decisions, and even take over the family businesses. This served as an important turning point in the daily lives of women in America.

20. False   The Constitution stated that when slaves ran away to a free area (one that did not have legal slavery), they still remained slaves, and their owners could claim them anywhere in the country.

# LESSON TWO

# LETTERS, WE GET LETTERS...

## Objectives:

☛ Students will identify American colonists' grievances against King George.
☛ Students will list grievances suffered by women, Native Americans, and African Americans during the late colonial period.
☛ Students will demonstrate letter-writing skills.

## Time: 2 or 3 class periods

## Materials:

✄ Social Studies textbook or other reference source
✄ Handout for each student:  "Grievances Against King George" and "Great Grievances"  (pages 128 and 129)

## Procedures:

1. Lead the class through a study of the Declaration of Independence. Pay particular attention to the section which lists grievances against King George III. Discuss these grievances.  Students make a list of those which are the most important on the handout entitled "Grievances Against King George."  The teacher may model this activity with an overhead projector and handout transparency.

2. Ask students to think of any grievances that African Americans, Native Americans, and women might have had during this period in history. Students write their ideas on the handout entitled "Great Grievances."

3. Following this, each student takes on the role of a member of one of the three groups mentioned above, and writes a letter to Thomas Jefferson.  Letters should detail specific grievances and offer solutions for a new nation to begin as one that endorses the concept that "all people are created equal."

4. Letters can be written on parchment-colored paper, the edges torn and rubbed with shoe polish to make them look "antique," and mounted for display.

## Assessment:

After the worksheets "Grievances Against King George" and "Great Grievances" are completed as a class, the teacher can circulate and quickly check that each student has completed them.

To evaluate the student letters, the teacher may use the rubric "Student Writing Rubric: Problem Solving Assignments," which is included in the Assessment Appendix on page 217.

## Why This Lesson?

Previously, students might have been asked to write letters to King George from the viewpoint of an American Patriot, listing grievances as mentioned in the Declaration of Independence. These grievances, however, were those perceived by the landowners and merchants of that time, and not representative of the entire population of the colonies. In this lesson, students have the opportunity to step into the shoes of someone else, gain some knowledge of what this person might have been going through during colonial times, and use this knowledge in a creative form of expression.

**Grievances against King George**

1.

2.

3.

4.

5.

6.

7.

8.

9.

Signed, _____
*(your signature)*
this_____day of _____in the year_____

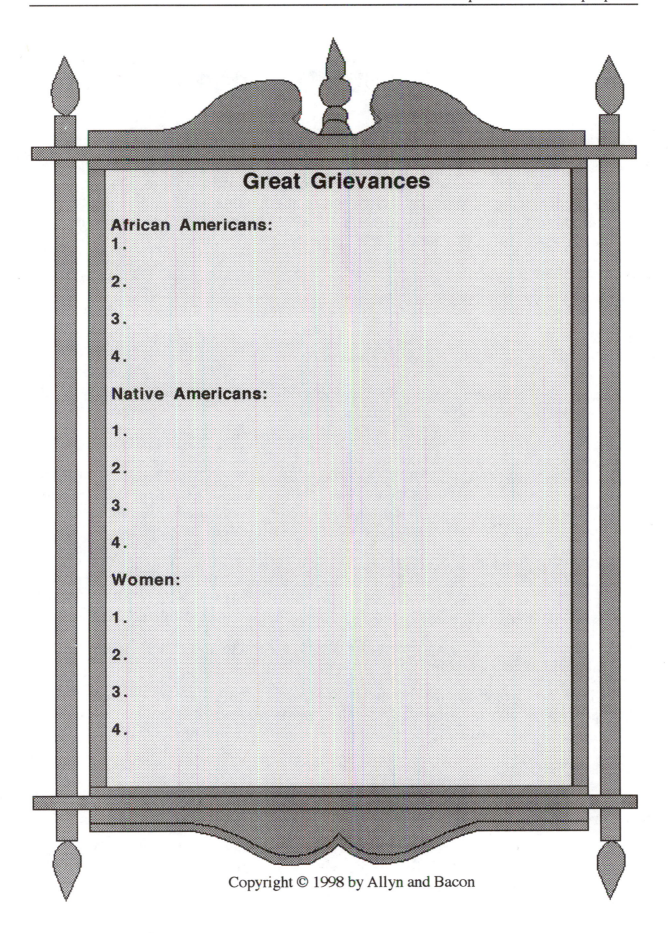

# Great Grievances

**African Americans:**

1.

2.

3.

4.

**Native Americans:**

1.

2.

3.

4.

**Women:**

1.

2.

3.

4.

# LESSON THREE

# PRESENTING OUR PREAMBLE

## Objectives:

☞ Students will discuss the preamble to the Constitution of the United States.

☞ Students will apply the wording and the intent of the preamble to diverse groups of people living within the United States at that time.

☞ Students will create a class preamble which applies to all students and incorporates an appreciation for acceptance and diversity.

## Time: 2 or 3 class periods

## Materials:

✄ Dictionaries
✄ Butcher paper for creating classroom banner
✄ Markers or crayons
✄ Handouts for each student: "The Preamble to the Constitution" and "We the People...But Which People?" (pages 131 and 132)

## Procedures:

1. The class reads and discusses the preamble to the Constitution. Students complete the handout entitled "The Preamble to the Constitution" in small groups, use dictionaries to define unfamiliar words, and attempt to explain the meaning of each phrase. The teacher may model this activity.

2. Next, using the handout entitled "We The People... But Which People?" the students take each phrase of the preamble, discuss it in groups, and write why this phrase couldn't have applied to African Americans, white servants, Native Americans, and women. The teacher may model this activity as well.

3. The class brainstorms the wording for a class preamble and votes on the phrases they would like to adopt.

4. After the new preamble is written, divide the class into 8 separate groups. Have each group take a section of the class preamble, write it on a large piece of butcher paper, illustrate it, and hang it up on the walls of the classroom.

## Assessment:

After the handouts are completed as a class, the teacher can circulate and quickly check that each student has completed them.

To assess cooperation in the creation of a class preamble, the teacher may use the "Rubric for Working Toward the Achievement of Group Goals" included in the Assessment Appendix on page 218.

## Why This Lesson?

The preamble to the Constitution is one of the best known and most memorized pieces of documentation in our country. Seldom does one stop and realize that the preamble, in all of its flowery wordiness, really did not apply to everyone living in the United States at that time. Students have the opportunity to see which, if any, portions of the preamble applied to everyone. Creating a class preamble could lead to a class Constitution and system of government.

## The Preamble To the Constitution

| Phrase from the Preamble | What does it mean? |
|---|---|
| We the people of the United States... | |
| ...in order to form a more perfect union... | |
| ...establish justice... | |
| ...ensure domestic tranquility... | |
| ...provide for the common defense... | |
| ...promote the general welfare... | |
| ...and secure the blessings of liberty to ourselves and our posterity... | |
| ...do ordain and establish this Constitution for the United States of America. | |

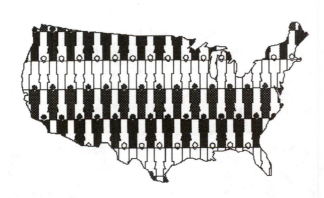

## WE THE PEOPLE...BUT WHICH PEOPLE?

| Phrase from the Preamble | Who benefited? | Who didn't? |
|---|---|---|
| We the people of the United States... | | |
| ...in order to form a more perfect union... | | |
| ...establish justice... | | |
| ...ensure domestic tranquility... | | |
| ...provide for the common defense... | | |
| ...promote the general welfare... | | |
| ...and secure the blessings of liberty to ourselves and our posterity... | | |
| ...do ordain and establish this Constitution for the United States of America. | | |

# LESSON FOUR

# INHERIT THE WIND

## Objectives:

☛ Students will discuss the Bill of Rights.
☛ Students will compare and contrast the Bill of Rights to the rights either enjoyed or denied by women, African Americans, and Native Americans in the late 18th century.
☛ Students will each create their own Bill of Rights.

## Time: about 3 class periods

## Materials:

✄ Social Studies textbook or other research materials about the Bill of Rights.
✄ Handout for each student: "The Bill of Rights: Was it for all?" (page 134)
✄ Handout for each student: "My Bill of Rights for Everyone" (page 135)

## Procedures:

1. Distribute the handout entitled "The Bill of Rights... Was it for all?".

2. Divide the class into ten small groups. Assign each group to read one of the amendments. Have groups prepare a short explanation concerning the origins and meaning of that amendment. As each group presents its amendment, the other students write it down in their notebooks.

3. When all ten amendments have been presented, the students work in groups to complete their notes to include in their "We the people...but which people" folders. Students should check off whether or not each of these amendments applied to and protected women, Native Americans, and African Americans. Discuss their ideas as a whole class.

4. Have each student create his/her own Bill of Rights, using the "My Bill of Rights" handout. Students describe individual rights that should protect all people in our country. Students can share what they have written.

## Assessment:

"The Bill of Rights: Was it For All?" handout is completed in small groups with class discussion. The teacher can circulate to check that students have completed this form accurately.

To assess the students' ability to create their own personal Bill of Rights, the teacher may use the "Rubric for Choosing Alternatives to Meet the Established Criteria," included in the Assessment Appendix on page 219.

## Why this Lesson?

The Bill of Rights is often presented as a "gift" that assures the American people of their individual rights.  Seen in the context of the times in which this document was written, it is important for students to realize that everyone in the United States was not a recipient of this "gift."

By composing an individual Bill of Rights, students can apply their new knowledge to create a document from which all citizens can benefit.

## Extension:

The teacher might want to extend this lesson by having students research whether the three groups of people in the lesson enjoy the rights today that were denied them at the time that the Bill of Rights was written. This could lead to study and discussion of the other sixteen amendments to the Constitution.

## The Bill of Rights...Was it for all?

# Amendment

## Does this amendment protect the following people? How?  Or why not?

**African Americans:**

**Native Americans:**

**Women:**

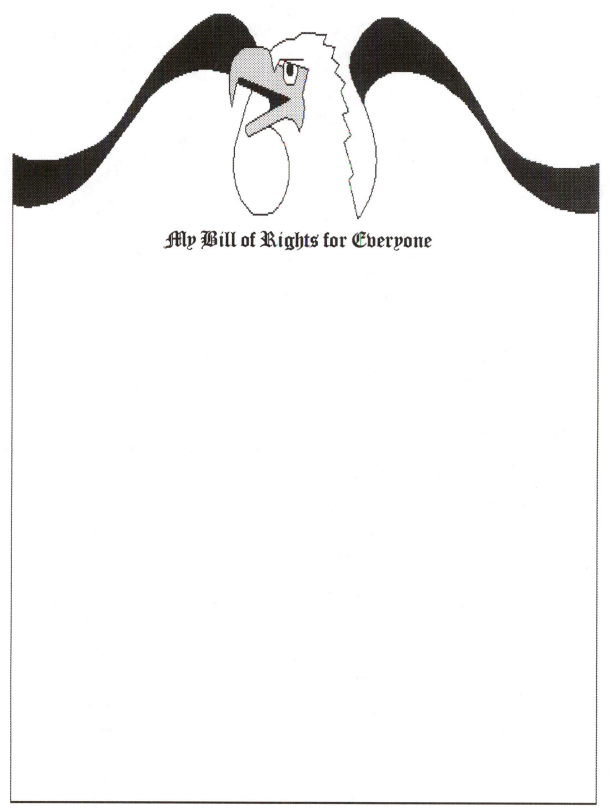

## My Bill of Rights for Everyone

## LESSON FIVE

## THE HAVES vs. THE HAVE NOTS

## Objectives:

☛ Students will demonstrate math skills involving addition, subtraction, multiplication, and division of whole numbers and fractions.

☛ Students will demonstrate cooperative teamwork.

**Time:** One class period

## Materials:

✂ The Haves vs. the Have Nots Math Game Handout for each student (pages 138 and 139)

✂ The Haves vs. the Have Nots Answer Key (page 137)

✂ The Haves vs. the Have Nots Math Game" on a transparency

✂ Overhead projector

✂ Two pieces of construction paper, cut into 6" by 6" squares (20 of each color)

✂ Scratch paper for each student

## Procedures:

1. Divide the class into two teams, the Haves and the Have Nots. Explain that you have chosen these names for the teams because at the end of the 18th century in the United States, there were definitely two groups of people: those who were privileged and endowed with many individual rights (the Haves), and those who weren't (the Have Nots).

2. Each team gets a set of 20 numbered squares of construction paper. The numbers run from 0 to 9. The Haves receive one color, the Have Nots receive the other. These are the numbers on the squares (and quantity of each digit) that you will need to make for each team.
   0 ( 5 )    1 ( 2 )    2 ( 1 )    3 ( 1 )    4 ( 1 )
   5 ( 2 )    6 ( 2 )    7 ( 1 )    8 ( 1 )    9 ( 1 )

3. Have one member of each team divide the teams' cards as evenly as possible among the members of the team.

4. Each team chooses two people to go up to the front of the room with scratch paper and a pencil. They will have to give their cards to other members of their team for that round.

5. The teacher, using the overhead projector, flashes one of the word problems on the board, reading it aloud at the same time. The two teams quickly get to work trying to solve the problem. When the members of one team think they have the answer, they silently go back to the rest of their team and point to

the team members that are holding the digits that they need. These team members quickly go up to the front of the room and are lined up in the proper order for the answer by the two students who computed the problem.

6. If the teacher looks at the answer and responds by a shake of the head, it means that the answer is not correct, and the two students must go back and try to rework the problem.

7. As soon as the teacher says, "That's correct!" the team that first correctly solved the problem gets one point.

8. The first team to get ten points wins!!

## Assessment:

The teacher can use observation to ascertain the facility with which the students are able to solve the given math problems. More instruction may be necessary in any areas where confusion and/or weakness are observed.

The teacher may use the "Cooperative Groupwork Observation Checklist" to evaluate the teamwork displayed by the competing groups. The checklist is included in the Assessment Appendix on page 220.

## Why This Lesson?

This is a fun way to present information to students, rather than in a lecture or read outloud. It is one way to pull together facts and figures concerning the unit being taught, while still holding the children's' interest.

**Note:** This lesson was adapted from a game entitled "The Americans vs. the British," in a thematic unit for teachers: The Revolutionary War, by John and Pattey Carratello, (Teacher Created Materials, Inc., 1991).

**Answer Key for The Haves vs. the Have Nots Math Game**

| | | | | | |
|---|---|---|---|---|---|
| 1. 6,000 | 2. 27 | 3. 56 | 4. 55 | 5. 75% | 6. 40% |
| 7. 1,676 | 8. 300 | 9. 267 | 10. 1,500,000 | 11. 1790 | 12. 11 |
| 13. $10^6$ | 14. 1,900 | 15. 19 | 16. 112 | 17. 520 | 18. 40% |
| 19. 20 | 20. 5,000 | | | | |

# The Haves
## vs.
# The Have Nots
## Math Game
Copyright © 1998 by Allyn and Bacon

1. In the King Philip's War of 1675-76, **3,712 + 428 +999 + 861**  Native Americans died from combat and disease.

2. In 1735, **393 - 57- 50 - 259**   Pequot chiefs complained to the governor of Connecticut that English settlers had moved onto their lands.

3. **8 x 7 x 3 x 2 ÷ 6** men were signers of the Declaration of Independence.

4. **10 x 10 x 10 - 930 - 15**  men were signers of the Constitution.

5. **15 x 20 ÷ 4 x 1** percent of the colonists who came to Virginia were indentured servants in the 17th century.

6. **160 x 1/4**  percent of the total population of Virginia in 1750 were African Americans.

7. In the year **5225 - 3549,** an armed rebellion of black slaves and white indentured servants was suppressed by the Virginia army.  It became known as Bacon's Rebellion.

8. **10 x 10 x 30 ÷ 10**   acres of land (plus one slave) were awarded to each white man who enlisted to fight in the American Revolution.

9. Thomas Jefferson owned **4 x 4 x 4 x 4 + 6 + 5** slaves in 1800.

10. There were **6,950,000 - 5,450,000** slaves in the United States at the end of the 18th century.

11. The Naturalization Act passed by Congress in the year **15 x 15 x 10 - 460** limited citizenship to white males who had lived in the United States for at least 2 years.

12. **121 ÷11** treaties were signed by Native American tribes in the early 1800's, ceding their land to the US government.

13. There were  **10 x 10 x 10 x 10 x 10 x 10** Native Americans living in North America when the Europeans first came.

14. There were __10 x 10 x 10 x 2 - 100__ Native American languages spoken before the coming of the Europeans.

15. In 1920, after the passage of the __1592 - 1314 - 259__ amendment, women obtained the right to vote in the United States.

16. It took __62 + 42 + 8__ days for a slave ship to travel from Africa to America.

17. __52 x 10__ slave uprisings were historically recorded as occurring in the United States.

18. __2,619 - 1763 - 250 - 475 - 91__ percent of white women in America who could read in 1750 (as compared to 90 percent for white males).

19. The slave trade continued for __14, 784 ÷ 4 ÷ 6 - 16 ÷ 30__ years after the ratification of the Constitution before being outlawed.

20. __1,500 x 3 + 500__ African American slaves fought for the Patriots in the American Revolution.

= + - = + - = + - = + - = + - = + - = + - = + - = + - = + -

(scratch area)

# LESSON SIX

# TUNEFUL BIOGRAPHIES

## Objectives:

☛ Students will demonstrate the ability to sing "Yankee Doodle" to the correct tune.
☛ Students will examine the life of a famous woman, African American, or Native American of the late 18th century.
☛ Students will create songs about famous people to the tune of "Yankee Doodle."
☛ Students will sing their songs to the rest of the class.

## Time: 2-3 class periods, and homework time for the students.

## Materials:

✂ Handouts for each student: "Famous Americans of the Times" and "Yankee Doodle: Composing a Biographical Tune" (pages 141 and 142)
✂ Reference sources for research

## Procedures:

1. Distribute a copy of "Yankee Doodle" to each student. Explain that this song was actually composed by the British during the Revolutionary War as a put-down of the Patriot forces. However, the song caught on with the Patriots and became their "anthem" during the war. The class should sing the song together, so that everyone is familiar with the tune.

2. Distribute copies of "Famous Americans of the Times." Students choose one of the individuals on the list and search for biographical information about that person. Why is s/he considered famous? What did s/he do during that period of history that is important? The teacher may provide reference materials for the class and allow time for the research. However, make it clear that the public library is a good place to obtain information. Give the students a due date for completing the research.

3. When all information has been collected, the students can begin working on their biographical songs to the tune of "Yankee Doodle." This activity is fun to do in class because the students enjoy bouncing their ideas and catchy phrases off one another.

4. When tunes are composed, students can sing them to the class and provide any other information about their famous person that wasn't in the song.

## Assessment:

Through practice and listening, teacher can assess the students' abilities to sing "Yankee Doodle" and carry the correct tune.

The teacher may use the "Student Writing Rubric: Providing Information on a Given Topic" to assess the ability of the students to conduct biographical research. The rubric is included in the Assessment Appendix on page 223.

The teacher can use the "Checklist for Student Performance: Yankee Doodle" to assess the ability to create a biographical song to the tune of "Yankee Doodle." The checklist is included in the Assessment Appendix on page 221.

## Why This Lesson?

Usually students are asked to research Revolutionary War heroes and those involved in the writing of the Declaration of Independence and the Constitution (all white males).  This lesson adds new perspectives and makes students aware that many people were instrumental in shaping our history.

# Famous Americans of the Times

| Women | African Americans | Native Americans |
|---|---|---|
| Abigail Adams | Crispus Attucks | Joseph Brant |
| Anne Bailey | Jean-Baptiste Mars Belley | |
| Penelope Barker | Martial Besse | Red Jacket |
| Elizabeth Champe | Austin Dabney | Tecumseh |
| Margaret Corbin | William Flora | |
| Lydia Darragh | James Forten | |
| Nancy Hart | Agrippa Hull | |
| Mary Ludwig Hays | George Latchom | |
| Hannah Hendee | William Lee | |
| Sybil Ludington | James Armistead Lafayette | |
| Mary L. Murray | Saul Matthews | |
| Mary Pickersgill | Peter Salem | |
| Phebe Reynolds | Joseph Ranger | |
| Betsy Ross | Caesar Tarrant | |
| Deborah Sampson | Prince Whipple | |
| Sally Townsend | Benjamin Bannecker | |
| Mercy Otis Warren | Prince Hall | |
| Phillis Wheatley | Paul Cuffe | |
| Tempe Wick | | |
| Betty Zane | | |

## "YANKEE DOODLE DANDY"
## Composing a Biographical Tune

Yankee Doodle went to town,
Riding on a pony,
He stuck a feather in his cap,
And called it macaroni.
Yankee Doodle keep it up,
Yankee Doodle dandy,
Mind the music and the step,
And with the girls be handy.


Now it's your turn! (Using the information you found on your Famous American of the Time, compose a "Tuneful Biography" to the tune of "Yankee Doodle.")

# LESSON SEVEN

# GREAT GAZETTES

## Objectives:

☛ Students will identify the "Five W's" of good reporting.
☛ Students will apply these skills to their own writing.

**Time:** 1 to 2 class periods (depending on how much time the teacher wishes to spend on review of newspaper articles) and homework time for the students.

## Materials:

✄ Handout for each student: "The Five 'W's of Good Reporting" (on page 144)
✄ Handout for each student: "Gazette" (on page 145)
✄ One or more recent newspaper articles which illustrate the "Five W's" of good reporting

## Procedures:

1. Review the "Five W's" (who, what, when, where, and why) of good reporting. Distribute copies of recent newspaper articles which illustrate the "Five W's" in the text. Students read the article(s) silently, and then underline each of the "Five W's" as it is found. Each student completes the handout entitled "The Five W's of Good Reporting." The class discusses its findings.

2. Distribute the gazette handout and explain that each student will be writing and illustrating the front page of a gazette as it might have appeared in the late 18th century. Students give their gazette a name, and date it. Then, several short articles are to be written (each having a headline), telling about situations involving women, Native Americans, or African Americans at that time. Sample headlines might include: "Boston Women Demand Entry to Harvard," "Native American Chiefs Ask the President for Their Land Back," " Slaves Demand Freedom for Fighting in the War." Articles may be based on events that happened, or may be fictionalized. Two illustrations should accompany the articles. Students are to follow the guidelines of the "Five W's" as they write.

3. Once backed on construction paper, these gazettes will make a beautiful bulletin board. The teacher can also bind them together for a class book.

## Assessment:

The teacher may use the "Rubric for Assessing Knowledge of the Five W's" to quickly evaluate understanding of the elements of good reporting. The rubric is included in the Assessment Appendix on page 222.

The teacher may use the "Student Writing Rubric: Providing Information on a Given Topic" as a means of assessing the gazette articles. The rubric is included in the Assessment Appendix on page 223.

## Why This Lesson?

Students have the opportunity to take knowledge they have acquired throughout this unit and apply it in a creative way. The history of that time is often portrayed from a white male perspective. The different viewpoints presented by the students should offer a fresh outlook on that period.

## Extension:

The teacher may want to use the newspaper to teach the concept of editorial cartooning to the class. Students can then draw an editorial cartoon in place of one of the illustrations required in the gazette.

---

# The Five W's of Good Reporting

Name: _____     Date: _____

## DIRECTIONS:

*Read the assigned newspaper article carefully. Underline the words or sentences that illustrate each of the five "W's" of good reporting.*

Name of the newspaper: _____

Date of the article: _____     Page where it appears: _____

Headline of the article: _____

## IDENTIFY THE FOLLOWING:

1. WHO is the article about?

2. WHAT is the article about?

3. WHEN does this news take place?

4. WHERE is this happening?

5. WHY is this happening?

---

# A GREAT GAZETTE

DATE _____ PRICE

TITLE

MAIN HEADLINE

CAPTION

HEADLINE

HEADLINE

# LESSON EIGHT

# IN THEIR SHOES

## Objectives:

☛ Students will examine situations that might have occurred to African Americans, women, and Native Americans at the end of the 18th century.

☛ Students will simulate these situations by writing, performing, or creating a product in cooperative groupwork.

**Time:** Teacher discretion

## Materials:

✂ Handout for each student: "In Their Shoes" (included on pages 147 to 149)

## Procedures:

1. Give each student a copy of "In Their Shoes," and explain that these are situations in which African Americans, Native Americans, and women may have found themselves at the end of the 18th century. Read over the situations and ensure that students realize the implications of each.

2. This lesson is designed so that the teacher can use several approaches, such as:

   📖 prompts for journal writing,

   📖 scenarios for debate teams or discussion groups,

   📖 springboards for student-created reader's theater scripts,

   📖 stimuli for student-created plays or poetry writing,

   📖 scenarios for "newscasts" in which the characters are interviewed,

   📖 dramas for "talk shows" in which the characters present their problems and seek feedback from an audience, and

   📖 prompts for writing "Dear Abby" letters describing a character's situation. Then students exchange letters and answer each other as "Abby."

## Assessment:

The teacher may want to choose one of the rubrics, scoresheets, or checklists presented in the Assessment Appendix depending on the simulation used.

## Why This Lesson?

Simulations are an excellent means of teaching and learning because the students can experience the feelings and hardships of others. Students internalize the material and view the situations from several different perspectives. The teacher is encouraged to use as many of the situations as possible, and create new ones.

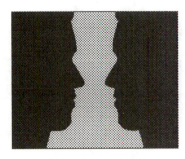

# In Their Shoes:

# African Americans

Copyright © 1998 by Allyn and Bacon

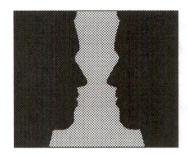

1. Your owner wants you to go and fight in the Revolutionary War in his place.  He says that he will give you your freedom when the war is over.  You're not sure you can trust him, and you don't even know if you will survive the war!  What will you do?

2. You fought on the side of the British during the Revolutionary War.  You have been freed from slavery, but you are also being banished from the United States for taking up the Loyalist cause.  Where will you go?

3. Your owner is going to break up your family, sending your brother to one plantation, your mother and father to another, and keeping you where you are. He is a kindly man, but thinks more about his land and money than he does his slaves.  You are wondering what to do.

4. You were very excited when the Declaration of Independence was written, and you heard that "all men are created equal."  You hope you will be freed soon and will have the same rights as everyone else.  You are devastated to hear about the new Constitution, and to learn that not only are you still a slave, but you are counted as only 2/3 of a white person and cannot vote.  You are angry and disappointed.  What can you do?

5. You want to learn to read, realizing that it is the ticket to respect and a livelihood when and if you are ever freed.  You know that you can be punished and even severely beaten if anyone finds out. One of your owner's children who you are friendly with sympathizes and offers to help you. There is a good chance that she will get into trouble, too, if discovered.  Is it worth the risk?  What do you do?

6. Your brother is trying to convince you to run away and seek freedom in the northern states.  You know that if you are caught, you will be punished and beaten and returned to your owner, and very few slaves have succeeded in escaping.  You have enough to eat on the plantation, and although you work very hard and are a slave, you have never known anything else.  Is it worth the risk?

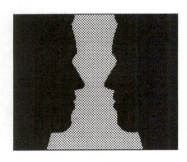

# In Their Shoes:
# Native Americans

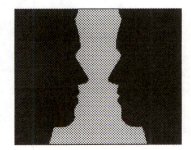

Copyright © 1998 by Allyn and Bacon

1. You are the chief of a well-known and respected tribe. You have been approached by both the Loyalists and the Patriots and asked to have your tribe fight on their sides. What will you do?

2. You have been asked by the United States government to move off your fertile land, where your tribe has lived for generations, and move to land that is less fertile, with little water. You know that if you resist, you and your tribe may lose everything, even your lives. What will you do?

3. You are preparing to take a journey to visit the President of the United States to speak to him about the wrongs you feel are taking place against your people. How will you express yourself? What will you tell him? Remember that you speak little English.

4. Your brother wants to attack a new white village that has settled on and taken over a large piece of your tribal land. You're not sure that violence is the best method, especially since the United States government takes terrible revenge on Native Americans who attack white settlers. How will you respond to your brother?

5. You have been asked to send your children to a white school to learn to read and write. Although you recognize the importance of their learning English, you are afraid they will lose their cultural identity and heritage. What will you do?

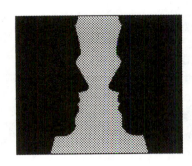

# In Their Shoes:

# Women

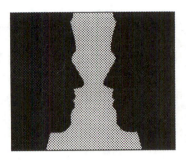

1. You have come to the battlefield to bring food and water to the Patriot troops. A soldier is wounded and falls. You know how to use a musket, but women are not allowed to be involved in battle. What will you do?

2. You have been asked to spy on Loyalist sympathizers. If caught, the charges of treason are punishable by death. You are invited to a party at the home of the governor, and you know there will be a lot of Loyalists there. You are a true believer in the Patriot cause, but are not sure you want to lose your life. What will you do?

3. You firmly believe that women should be allowed equal rights with men. You are very angry that you are not allowed to vote. You also feel that women should be represented in Congress by women. What steps can you take?

4. The African American slave who has taken care of you since you were a baby asks you to help hide her brother, who has just run away from his owner in the neighboring town. That owner was cruel, and he fed and clothed his slaves poorly. You want to help, but you know you, your slave, and her brother could face terrible consequences if caught. What will you do?

5. Your father has just told you that you cannot go to a university like your brother did. "It's not for women," he states. You want to become a great mathematician, and you know that you require much more education. However, no women that you know have ever learned more than basic reading and writing. What will you do?

6. You are an indentured servant who has two more weeks of servitude left, but no money. You desperately need to pay bail for your brother, who was jailed for stealing a loaf of bread. Your master will give you $200 if you will serve another five years. What will you do?

# Summary and Suggestions

I feel it is important for teachers to present the primary source materials of the time, so that children can get a better feel for the thoughts and feelings of the diverse groups of people that populated the United States at this period of history. Examples are: the poetry of Phillis Wheatley, letters written by Abigail Adams to her husband (as well as his responses!), the writings of Benjamin Bennaker, letters written by Native American chiefs protesting treatment by white settlers, and statements taken by African American slaves and white indentured servants of the time. Excellent sources for these writings are The Free and the Unfree by Peter N. Carroll and David W. Noble (1978), A Different Mirror by Ronald Takaki (1993), A People's History of the United States by Howard Zinn (1980), Voices in African American History: The American Revolution published by Modern Curriculum Press, and the Treasury of American Poetry, edited by Nancy Sullivan. (A complete listing is available in the Reference section of this unit.) Only by reading the actual words of persons living during the late colonial period can students appreciate the feeling and passions which motivated action and resulted in the subsequent course of history.

There are several songs I have on audiotape: one about slavery, one on indentured servitude, one a woman's lament after her husband leaves for war, and one on the differences between male and female roles at that time. These would be wonderful to introduce to the class for singing, discussion, and for comparison with contemporary music and lyrics. The audiotape is by Steven Traugh (1994) and is entitled Voices of American History, Vol. I: Pre-colonial times through the Revolutionary War. It is published by Creative Teaching Press, Inc. in Cypress, CA 90630.

After looking through this unit, I realized that students might have difficulty finding biographical information on the "famous" people mentioned in the "Tuneful Biographies" lesson, since the literature and reference materials may not adequately reflect the trend toward more diverse representation in teaching and curriculum. The teacher might have to search out the necessary information, copy it and provide it for the class.

There is, however, one word of caution which goes along with this project. This unit can only be successful if students, since the beginning of the year, have been exposed to an education which stresses diversity and acceptance. Students should, before this unit begins, already be aware of the effect of the European invasion on the Native Americans, and the inception of the slave trade into the colonies, as well as indentured servitude. This unit will have little meaning or lasting impact if taught in a vacuum.

I love history...I feel that students need to know where they came from in order to understand where they are going. However, I also feel that in the past, students were not given a true representation of the history they were expected to study. Hopefully, this unit will help to remedy that situation in a practical and interesting way.

## Personal Profile

I'm a fifth grade teacher at the Mary Bergeson elementary school in Laguna Niguel, California. It's a suburban school that draws its population from a wide range of socio-economic levels: from blue collar parents to professionals. The school might not be considered "diverse" in the traditional sense because it is predominantly Caucasian and doesn't have a large Latino or African American population. However, there is a growing Asian population in the school and quite a large Persian community.

My interest in multicultural education has come out of feeling myself to be in a minority as a Jewish woman. Additionally, throughout their schooling, my sons have felt some discomfort in being Jewish in a public educational system which is distinctly Christian. So, for cultural as well as religious reasons I have wanted my classroom to be inclusive. In addition to the intellectual argument that cultural diversity is the way of the world, I have wanted every one of my students to feel comfortable that who they are and what they are about was valued and respected by me.

Two of my main interests, outside of school, are British and American history, and I have a strong belief that we need to know where we have come from as a nation in order to understand where we are going. The "old" history was one-sided in its view of events. I am convinced that students need an awareness of the truth--the whole picture-- in order to become informed citizens and participate fully in our country's future.

# CHAPTER SEVEN

## Maya and Aztec: A study of the ancient Mexican civilizations

### by Karen Kellogg

I teach sixth grade "Core" -- a combination of social science and language arts, and the California curriculum framework at my level focuses on ancient civilizations. While a large number of my students are from Mexico, I found it quite disappointing that our social science book somehow left out any mention of the great ancient Mexican civilizations. I believe that it is very important and necessary for me to show my students the value and worth of their ancestors. It was from this belief that I decided to develop my own unit on the civilizations of the Maya and Aztecs.

I prefer to take an integrated hands-on approach in my teaching of these two subject areas. So the literature I use comes from the stories (myths and legends) of that civilization as well as historical fiction set in that time period. Through integration and hands-on learning, my students gain an understanding of and appreciation for each civilization we study. The lessons in this chapter comprise a three-week unit on the Maya and Aztecs, two powerful ancient Mexican civilizations. To give my students a close look at these civilizations, I chose to focus on one particular aspect of the culture (i.e. religion, food sources) every day or two, and I tried to come up with something hands-on that would help them to remember its significance. I also chose to create a mini-literature unit based on a legend from Mesoamerica, "A Tale of Chocolate", as a way to share some of the beliefs important to these groups of people.

By highlighting one civilization at a time, the unit adopts a Single-Group Studies approach. One of the main ideas of this approach is to empower oppressed groups. It was noted in Sleeter and Grant's <u>Making Choices for Multicultural Education</u> (1994), that ethnic studies should give students of color a sense of their history, increase their awareness, and build their self-confidence. I think Mexican students are empowered by learning about the great achievements of their ancestors.

This approach includes looking at the art, music, and cultural expressions of these people. We learn, by studying these aspects of Maya and Aztec culture, what a vital role religion played in their lives on a daily basis. It has taken many hours of research to develop this unit. It was time well spent in order to give my students a balanced introduction to these amazing civilizations and people.

# Quick View Chart of the Instructional Unit

| Lesson One<br>"Introduction and Background"<br><br>Students are introduced to the unit and construct a timeline of important dates. | Lesson Two<br>"Religion"<br><br>The importance of religion in Aztec life is examined, and students create a pyramid silhouette. |
|---|---|
| Lesson Three<br>"Family Life and Community"<br><br>Family roles, community life, and social organization are explored, and students cooperatively recreate a marketplace scene or a family life. | Lesson Four<br>"Food Sources"<br><br>Students share in the discovery of chocolate and conduct a class cooking activity. |
| Lesson Five<br>"Government"<br><br>The government structure is studied, and each student makes a warrior headdress. | Lesson Six<br>"Achievements in Art"<br><br>Various arts are focused upon and Mosaic masks are constructed. |
| Lesson Seven<br>"Music and Dance"<br><br>Instruments and rhythms are introduced. Students do the "Dance of the Reeds" using the mask and headdress they created. | Lesson Eight<br>"Sports and Games"<br><br>Students learn about sports and games and create their own rules for playing "patolli" (a board game similar to Parcheesi). |
| Lesson Nine<br>"Writing"<br><br>Mayan and Aztec writing are studied, and student partners create their own stories and "translate" them into hieroglyphs. | Lesson Ten<br>"Mayans Today"<br><br>The conquest and collapse of Mayan and Aztec civilizations are presented and discussed. A video is watched. |
| Lesson Eleven<br>"Passports and Review"<br><br>Students make a passport to organize and review the information learned. | Lesson Twelve<br>"Assessment of Student Learning"<br><br>An essay examination and the evaluation of student projects complete the unit. |

# LESSON ONE

# INTRODUCTION AND BACKGROUND

I have provided an overview to each lesson in the "Procedures" section which highlights the key points to be presented in that lesson. However, teachers should supplement with more detailed information.

## Objectives:

☛ Students will identify the American Indians and the Spanish as the two major civilizations in Mexican culture.
☛ Students will learn important dates.
☛ Students will construct a time line.

## Time: One day, approximately 2 to 3 hours

## Materials:

✄ Tom Snyder's Time line program (Mac and Apple IIe) or
✄ White copy paper, scissors, tape and markers
✄ Aztec and Maya Date Sheet (included on page 155)
✄ Maya and Aztec Project Evaluation Sheet (included on page 178)

## Procedures:

1. Begin by giving the basic background on ancient Mexican civilizations.

   **Overview:** Mexico is the result of two civilizations -- the American Indians and the Spanish. The first people in what is now called Mexico were the Indians. The Indian people formed tribes and built great civilizations. Two of these civilizations were the Maya and Aztecs. The Spanish arrived in Mexico in 1519 and conquered the most powerful tribe -- the Aztecs. Spain made a colony of Mexico and called it New Spain. Over the centuries the Spanish and the Indian people intermarried. There are many people in Mexico who call themselves Mestizos (Multicultural Mini-Units, 1993).

2. Using the Aztec and Maya Date Sheet on the following page, present major dates for both civilizations. Have each student create a time line (by computer program or by hand). Timelines should combine both civilizations to illustrate when each flourished and collapsed.

3. Introduce the assessments to be used both during and at the conclusion of the unit. Students should familiarize themselves with the "targets" of assessment and the criteria for evaluation.

## Assessment:

Evaluate timelines using the project evaluation sheet.

# Aztec and Maya Date Sheet

| Aztec Territory | Mayan Territory |
|---|---|
| | |

**900 A. D.**

An empire is established in the Valley of Mexico by Toltecs, a warlike tribe.

**3114 B. C.**

The date of the beginning of the Mayan calendar.

**1300 to 1400 A. D.**

The capital city of Tenochtitlan is constructed on an island in Lake Texcoco.

**1500-1000 B. C. to 150 A. D.**

Period of Mayan history when farming communities and some temples are established on the Yucatan peninsula.

**1440 to 1470 A. D.**

The Aztec King Montezuma I reigns and expands the empire to the south and east to the Gulf Coast.

**300 to 925 A. D.**

The Classic Period of Mayan civilization when writing, sculpture, architecture and other cultural expressions are developed.

**1500 to 1520 A. D.**

The Aztec Empire has reached its highest point of power. Montezuma II reigns.

**925 to 975 A. D.**

Approximate period in the tenth century when Mayan society began to decline.

**1520 A. D.**

The Spanish Army under the command of Hernán Cortés conquers the capital city of Tenochtitlan.

**1194 A. D.**

Chichen Itza, the capital city, falls to the Mayapan Indians, who rule harshly for many years.

**1620 A. D.**

The Spanish brought slavery and disease. By this date the Indian population had declined by 90 percent.

**1697 A. D.**

The Spanish commander, Martin de Ursaa, captures Tayasal, a jungle city where the remaining Maya have hidden since 1464.

# LESSON TWO

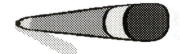

# RELIGION

## Objectives:

☛ Students will recall that religion touched almost every aspect of Mayan and Aztec life.

☛ Students will identify the basic characteristics and beliefs of the Mayan and Aztec religions.

☛ Students will construct pyramid silhouettes.

## Time: Two days, approximately 4 to 6 hours

## Materials:

✂ Overhead transparency of Mayan and Aztec gods (included on page 158)
✂ Watercolors and brushes for each student
✂ White construction paper (8 1/2" x 11")
✂ Black construction paper (8 1/2" x 11")
✂ Scissors, glue
✂ Maya and Aztec Project Evaluation Sheet (included on page 178)

## Procedures:

1. Start the focal lessons by discussing religion, as it touched almost every aspect of Mayan and Aztec life.

   **Overview:** The ancient Maya were very religious, worshipping many gods. Many of the gods were tied in one way or another to agriculture. Religion played a large role in the Mayan culture, with each day of the year having some religious significance. They had ceremonies, festivals, rituals, and celebrations, all based on their many gods -- gods of rain, corn, sun, moon, medicine, weaving, and so on. Masks were used by Mesoamerican priests in ceremonial services to depict the various gods. Frequently, Quetzalcoatl (called Kukulcan by the Maya), a major god to the Aztec, was shown wearing a white or red mask. Other gods were depicted in other colors. Different Mesoamerican groups described these same gods in various ways, according to their own unique traditions.

   Religion was also a prominent part of the life of the Aztec people, and they, too, had many gods, including gods of agriculture. Their holidays were celebrations and ceremonies for the gods of rain, sun, corn, fire, spring, and regrowth. Like the Maya, Aztec priests used masks to depict the gods in ceremonies. Aztec religion was concerned with the sun. Aztecs believed that they lived in the era of the fifth sun and that one day the world would end violently. In order to postpone their destruction, men performed human sacrifices. Their duty was to feed the gods with human blood; thereby keeping the sun alive. Aztecs believed that when they died, they would go on living in another world. If a person died a normal death, his/her soul had to pass through the nine levels of the underworld before reaching Mictlan, the realm of the death god. Warriors who died in battle and women who died in childbirth joined the sun god in the sky (Teacher's Guide to A Quetzalcoatl Tale of Chocolate, 1994).

2. Show pictures on the overhead of various gods (included on the following page).

3. 6th graders will be interested in hearing about one particular type of religious ritual -- HUMAN SACRIFICE.

   **Background:** The Aztecs held special ceremonies that involved sacrifice in temples or on mountain tops. The Maya sometimes sacrificed victims in wells. Priests performed the sacrifices, which took place at important festivals throughout the year. The victims were men, women, and children -- sometimes animals. The Maya sometimes drowned their victims and the Aztecs removed the victim's heart. Human sacrifice was a communion with the gods: it was necessary to feed them to keep the cosmic order. People believed that just as the gods sacrificed themselves during the creation of the sun and the moon, they had to do the same (Aztec, Inca, and Maya, 1993).

4. Discuss how one of the many focal points for the religious rites was sacred buildings, or temples dedicated to the gods.

5. The teacher may want to set the stage for this activity by playing reed flute music and leading a guided visualization. Have students imagine coming through the jungle and seeing an Aztec city at sunset. Imagine the pyramids are black against a magnificent Mexican sunset. On a piece of white construction paper the students make a watercolor using reds and oranges. Have the students trace or free hand draw a temple pyramid on the black construction paper. Cut it out and glue it on top of the dried watercolor. Add cacti or whatever the imagination will allow. As an alternative, students may want to fingerpaint the background.

## Assessment:

Evaluate pyramid silhouettes using the project evaluation sheet on pages 178 and 224.

# Mayan and Aztec gods

| Mayan gods | Aztec gods |
|---|---|
| Kukulcan: Feathered Serpent | Quetzalcoatl: Feathered Serpent |
| Chac: god of rain | Tlaloc: god of rain |
| Itzamná: god of creation | Tezcatlipoca: god of creation |

# LESSON THREE

# FAMILY LIFE AND COMMUNITY

## Objectives:

☞ Students will list the characteristic roles and responsibilities within Aztec and Mayan households and communities.
☞ Students will work together cooperatively.
☞ Students will recreate Mayan marketplace or Aztec Family Life scenes.

**Time:** Two days, approximately 4 to 6 hours

## Materials:

✄ Role buttons (included on page 108 of <u>Maya, Aztecs, Incas</u>, 1994)
✄ K-W-L Chart (included on page 107 of <u>Maya, Aztecs, Incas</u>, 1994)
✄ Copies of the Mayan Marketplace and the Aztec Family Life Scenes and Facts (included on pages 56, 57, 58, and 59 of <u>Maya, Aztecs, Incas</u>, 1994)
✄ White copy paper (4 sheets per group)
✄ Tagboard
✄ Pencils, markers, scissors, yarn, glue or tape
✄ Maya and Aztec Project Evaluation Sheet (included on page 178)

## Procedures:

1. Discuss Family and Community.

> **Overview:** For the Maya, the social hierarchy had feudal lords who received tribute (produce and services) from the peasants. The nobility did not pay tribute. Clothing styles reflected a person's social class. For example, people who wore clothes of fine material with colorful and elaborate decoration were of higher status than those in less expensive clothing. At the marketplace, the center of the community, every sort of good was traded. Families brought crops and manufactured goods to barter for the goods they could not produce themselves. The husband was responsible for the well-being of his family and his government. The wife was in charge of the household, which included weaving, cooking, and raising children. Girls learned domestic chores from their mothers, and boys learned their father's trade. Children went to school to learn dances, songs, and about religious festivals. Noble children had their own schools where they learned astrology, how to read codices (Mayan books), and how to rule.

> The Aztec way of life was very similar to that of the Maya. People paid tribute to the government in the form of food, clothing, skins, gold, silver, and feathers -- whatever the family was able to hunt, trade, or produce themselves. Students may be interested in hearing how children were punished. From the age of 11 years, disobedient Aztec children were

punished in various ways by their parents.  Punishments included pricking their skin with spines and making them inhale chili smoke by holding them over a fire burning with chili peppers (Maya, Aztecs, Incas, 1994).

2. Introduce Cooperative Learning Activity:  Mural Scenes and Facts (Maya, Aztecs, Incas, 1994).  Students are put into a total of eight groups of 4 or 5.  Each student receives a role button to help remember his or her group job.  Four of the groups will focus on the Mayan Marketplace scene, and the other four will focus on the Aztec Family Life scene.

3. Groups are given either the Mayan Market Place or the Aztec Family Life scenes and facts.

4. Groups meet to establish what they **know** and **want to know** about the scene they have received.  Each group's "Tupil" records the group's responses on the K-W-L chart.

5. The cooperative groups create a mural.  This is a drawing activity where each group redraws a small section of a complete scene onto larger paper to make a cooperative display.  By working in four person groups, each group completes four sections of the scene on the four sheets of white copy paper.  The completed four sheets unite with those of the three other groups to create a larger sixteen section scene (approximately  36" x 44").  Students might want to divide their four sections into even smaller quarters, strips, or bands.  After redrawing the scene, the students cut the facts apart and place them around the edge of their part of the mural.  Next they  string colored yarn to connect the fact cards and the areas of the mural that the card describes.

6. When murals are completed, each group shares with the whole class their part of the drawing and the corresponding facts.

7. Each group then completes their K-W-L chart about what they **learned** from this activity.

## Assessment:

Evaluate mural scenes and facts using the project evaluation sheet on pages 178 and 224.

# LESSON FOUR

# FOOD SOURCES

## Objectives:

☛ Students will identify food sources of these civilizations.
☛ Students will recall lasting contributions of the Mayan and Aztec people.
☛ Students will memorize a story from the civilization and time period that helps us to gain knowledge of the people and their lives.
☛ Students will make Mexican hot chocolate.

## Time: Two days, approximately 4 to 6 hours

## Materials:

✄ Single or multiple copies of A Quetzalcoatl Tale of Chocolate by Marilyn Parke and Sharon Panik
✄ Word list (included on page 163)
✄ Ingredients for making Mexican hot chocolate (included on page 162)
✄ A molinillo (a wooden tool used to beat hot chocolate, or a single beater from an electric mixer)
✄ A hot plate
✄ A saucepan for heating milk
✄ A coffee mug or cup for each student
✄ Maya and Aztec Project Evaluation Sheet (included on page 178)

## Procedures:

1. Explain that food sources will be the next characteristic of these civilizations to be highlighted in class. The background information will expand on a literature mini-unit, entitled A Quetzalcoatl Tale of Chocolate.

   Overview: The Maya and Aztecs ate simply. Maize was the central food in their diet, supplemented by other vegetables, such as beans and squashes. They ate maize tortillas (pancakes) with every meal. Tamales were a favorite dish, which was a kind of envelope of steamed maize stuffed with vegetables or meat. There was also evidence of early use of chocolate by the Maya gathered in recent excavations at Rio Azul, Guatemala. Residue in some of the pottery there has been identified as chocolate. A Maya glyph for "Ka-ka-wa" (translated as "cacao") was found in a container. The Maya may have cultivated cacao on plantations as early as 600 AD. Chocolate was a popular drink in Aztec time, too. Earlier Indians discovered beans growing on wild cacao plants. As the Maya before them, the Aztec roasted and ground the beans into powder (choco). They mixed it with water (atl) and called the drink chocolatl. A hot chocolate drink was a luxury item for the Aztec and was probably exclusive to the nobility.

2. Read <u>A Quetzalcoatl Tale of Chocolate</u> to the class.  This legend had been a part of Mayan/Aztec culture.  Introduce new words within the context of the story as you read (word list included on the following page).

3. As an extension to this activity, have the class pantomime some of the words.  Or ask the students to think of synonyms for each word.

4. Ask the following questions to help guide a class discussion and to encourage critical thinking:  Why was chocolate so valued by the people of the earth?  How was it used?  How was the lifestyle of the Shining Jaguar clan similar to and different from your own?  Why was Two Wind Deer sent out of the temple?  What surprised you about the story?  Did you expect Two Wind Deer to become a hero?  Why or why not?  What are seven foods the "people of the earth" ate?  How does your diet compare to that of the Shining Jaguar clan?  Quetzalcoatl took the form of a monkey to help the people of the earth find chocolate.  In what other ways do you think Quetzalcoatl could have helped get chocolate for the people?

5. Independent Writing Activity: Have the students write their own legends of the origin of another food.  Share with classmates.

6. Make Mexican Hot Chocolate with the class.  The following recipe serves 4.  Multiply the ingredients as needed for the number of students in the class.  This would be a good math activity on the day before making the chocolate.

## Assessment:

Evaluate independent writing (personal legend) using the project evaluation sheet on pages 178 and 224.

---

### Mexican Hot Chocolate

4 cups of milk
5 1-ounce squares of chocolate
3 2-inch sticks of cinnamon
1 teaspoon of vanilla
Honey (optional)

Combine the milk, chocolate, and cinnamon sticks in a saucepan and heat.  Stir just until the chocolate melts.  Remove from the heat.  Then remove the cinnamon and stir in one teaspoon of vanilla.  Beat with the molinillo until frothy.  Serve in mugs with cinnamon stick stirrers.  Honey may be added, if desired.

---

# Word List
# for A Quetzalcoatl Tale of Chocolate

| | |
|---|---|
| cacao | squawks |
| atlatls | ashamed |
| scampered | illuminated |
| plaza | From *A Quetzalcoatl Tale of Chocolate* by Marilyn Parke and Sharon Panik. © 1994 by *Fearon Teacher Aids*, a division of American Teaching Aids. Used by permission. |

# LESSON FIVE

# GOVERNMENT

## Objectives:

☞ Students will identify the roles of Mayan and Aztec leaders.
☞ Students will recall the personal and civic responsibilities of individuals.
☞ Students will construct a warrior headdress.

## Time: One day, approximately 2 to 3 hours

## Materials:

✂ Glyph and feather patterns (included on page 165)
✂ 12" length of grosgrain ribbon or elastic, 1-1/2" to 2" wide (one per student)
✂ White tagboard, 8-1/2" by 11" sheet per student
✂ Stapler
✂ Scissors, glue gun and glue sticks (or fabric glue)
✂ Markers
✂ Maya and Aztec Project Evaluation Sheet (included on page 178)

## Procedures:

1.  Introduce the lesson by announcing that the focus will be on Mayan/Aztec Government.

    **Overview:** Maya and Aztec leaders had absolute power over all society. They were warriors, fighting for control of other cities. Leaders also served the needs of the people, seeing that they were well-fed and housed. Each individual had specific personal and civic responsibilities, be it as farmers, priests, soldiers, merchants, rulers, or crafts people.

2.  Students make a Warrior headdress which will be used in lesson nine for the Mayan Dance of the Reeds. Share the feather and glyph patterns with the students and have them trace or draw 6 to 8 feathers and 3 to 5 glyphs on the white tagboard. Cut out these shapes. The feathers and glyphs may be colored using markers. Have students measure each others' heads (perhaps a head size chart could be created as a math activity). Students cut the ribbon (or elastic) 1/2" longer than their head measurement. Staple the ribbon or elastic ends together to create a headband. Check to ensure the headband fits. Using the glue gun (teacher or parent volunteer may want to monitor this step in the procedures), affix the feathers to the back side of the headband and attach the glyphs to the front side. The headdress is complete.

## Assessment:

Evaluate headdresses using the project evaluation sheet on pages 178 and 224.

# Warrior Headdress Feathers and Glyphs

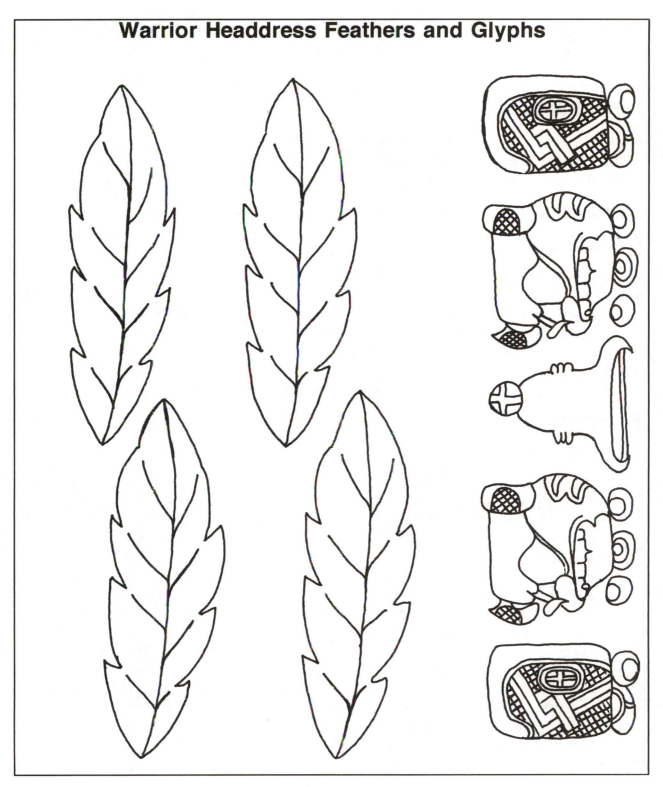

# LESSON SIX

# ACHIEVEMENTS IN ART

## Objectives:

☛ Students will identify a variety of Mayan and Aztec art forms.
☛ Students will recall the materials used in artistic expression.
☛ Students will recreate a mosaic mask.

**Time:** One day, approximately 2 to 3 hours

## Materials:

✂ Mask model (included on page 167)
✂ Assorted sheets of construction paper, colors coordinated to represent commonly used metals and stones (jade, turquoise, silver, gold, and so on)
✂ White tagboard, approximately 8-1/2" by 11" (one per student)
✂ Two 10" long strips of ribbon or string
✂ Scissors, glue
✂ Maya and Aztec Project Evaluation Sheet (included on page 178)

## Procedures:

1. Begin the lesson with a discussion of Mayan/Aztec achievements in art.

   **Overview:** Pottery and walls are today's best examples of Mayan painting, which were important to daily and ritual life of Maya society. Painters were highly educated and held positions of importance. Artists recorded history and mythology, one and the same with the Aztecs. Aztec artistic, religious, and technical achievements were based on the cultures of the Toltecs, Maya, and Zapotecs, earlier groups they conquered and displaced. The Aztec culture combined elements of these earlier civilizations. They developed a culture that included a stone wheel calendar; sculptures in hard and soft stone; buildings made with exceptional engineering skills; and jewelry made of jade, turquoise, and other semi-precious stones. Metal work included copper, silver, and gold. Almost every culture in the world has worn masks during festivals and ceremonies. The Maya and Aztecs were no exception. Masks were made of many materials , often inlaid with gold or gems. Masks were placed over mummies to protect them in the afterlife. Many were hung on walls in temples and worshipped (<u>Maya, Aztec, Incas</u>, 1994).

2. Using the mask model, students trace or draw the outline on tagboard. Have the students design the mask on graph paper with colored pencils by mixing colors and patterns. Then they cut the colored construction paper into small squares or irregular shaped pieces to glue onto the tagboard mask as mosaic tiles. Finally, staple the string or ribbon strips to each side of the mask as ties.

## Assessment:

Evaluate masks using the project evaluation sheet on pages 178 and 224.

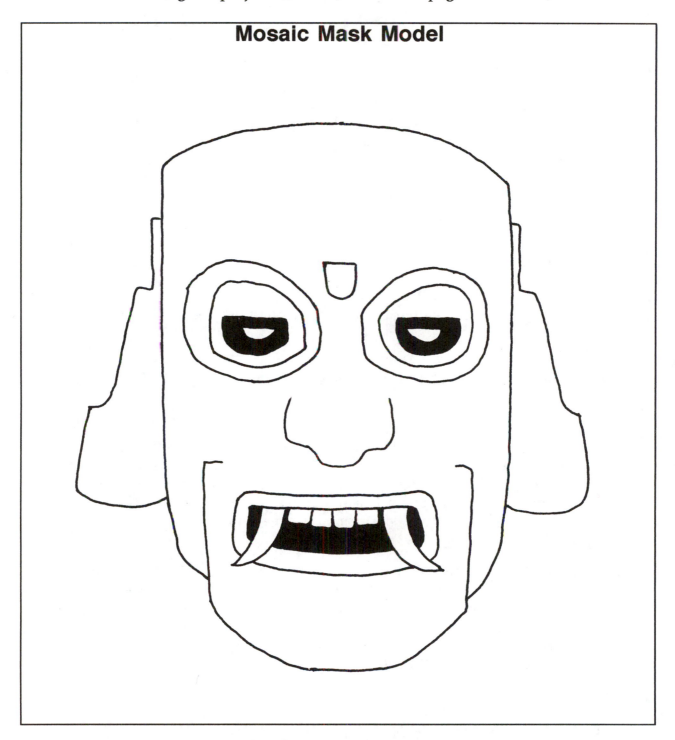

**Mosaic Mask Model**

Copyright © 1998 by Allyn and Bacon

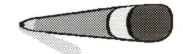

# LESSON SEVEN

# MUSIC AND DANCE

## Objectives:

☛ Students will identify the types of instruments utilized in the creation of music.

☛ Students will recall the significance of dance in these civilizations.

☛ Students will perform a dance wearing their masks and headdresses created in earlier lessons.

## Time: One day, approximately 2 to 3 hours.

## Materials:

✄ Students' masks

✄ Students' headdresses

✄ Drums, gourd and shell rattles

✄ Maya and Aztec Project Evaluation Sheet (included on page 178)

## Procedures:

1. Discuss how music, song, and dance were an important part of Mesoamerican life.

   **Overview:** The most common instruments were rattles, whistles, trumpets, flutes, copper bells, and shells. To these civilizations, music and dance were closely linked to religion. Everyone, from rulers to peasants, took part in dances and performed especially for their gods. Dances and games were performed in the Dance Court near the temple or in the marketplace. The Maya Dance of Reeds was performed by as many as 150 people at a time (Aztec, Inca, and Maya, 1993).

2. Have the students practice and then perform the Mayan Dance of Reeds. Two dancers are chosen to dance in the center of a circle. While these two dancers mime the parts of a hunter and a deer (or a hunted man), the other dancers circle to the left. Circle dancers sway toward the center of the circle and then away from the center with their arms stretching in and out to the beat of drums, gourds, and shell rattles.

## Assessment:

Evaluate Dance of the Reeds using the project evaluation sheet on pages 178 and 224.

# LESSON EIGHT

# SPORTS AND GAMES

## Objectives:

☛ Students will recognize the role of sports in Aztec and Maya life.
☛ Students will describe the games of Patolli and Pok-a tok.
☛ Students will invent rules and play their own versions of Patolli.

**Time:** One day, approximately 2 to 3 hours

## Materials:

✄ Patolli game board (included on page 170)
✄ Tagboard the size of the game to be played (11" by 18" is ideal)
✄ Colored markers
✄ Assorted odds and ends which may be used to decorate the boards or serve as game markers
✄ Maya and Aztec Project Evaluation Sheet (included on page 178)

## Procedures:

1. In the introduction to the lesson, discuss the fact that, as with every other aspect of Mesoamerican life, sports and games revolved around religion.

   **Overview:** Two main games played by the Aztecs were patolli, a board game similar to Parcheesi, and the ball game Pok-a Tok. Pok-a Tok was played in Mesoamerica long before the Aztecs by other ancient Mexican civilizations, such as the Maya. The ball court represented the world, and the ball stood for the moon and the sun. Bets were placed on the outcome of the game, and some players lost everything they had -- including their lives.

2. Students are introduced to the Patolli Cooperative Game Activity in which groups of 4 to 5 students are given a copy of the game board and are asked to invent rules for the game. Each group writes down the rules, draws and colors their game board on the large tagboard, and tests the play of the game with each other. Groups are to design and make the game markers and the method by which to advance along the board: throw of dice, spin of a number wheel, and so on. Each group shares their game with the class.

3. Leave the games on display for use during free time.

## Assessment:

Evaluate Patolli games using the project evaluation sheet on pages 178 and 224.

# PATOLLI GAME BOARD

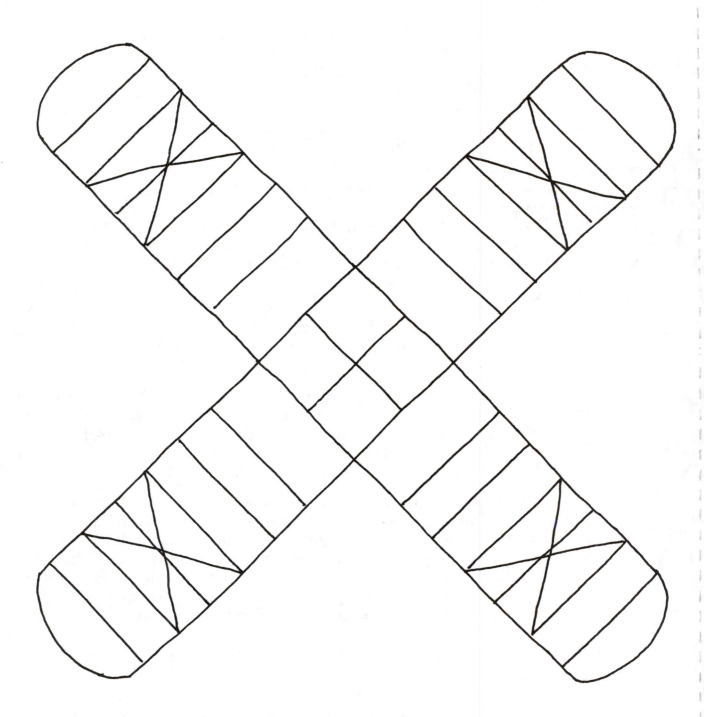

# LESSON NINE

# WRITING

## Objectives:

☞ Students will describe the writing systems of the Aztec and Maya.
☞ Students will recall the importance of numbers and time to these civilizations.
☞ Students will write a story, translate it into hieroglyphs, and create a codex.

**Time:** One day, approximately 2 to 3 hours

## Materials:

✄ Sample glyphs (included on page 172)
✄ Plenty of drawing paper
✄ Markers, glue, tape and scissors
✄ Heavy construction paper, taped and folded accordion-style
✄ Maya and Aztec Project Evaluation Sheet (included on page 178)

## Procedures:

1. Discuss their system of writing during this lesson.

   **Overview:** The Maya are the only people in ancient America who developed an original writing system, made paper from trees, and to use paper to make books. Of thousands of codices or folding screen books, all but four were destroyed by the Spanish. They used picture symbols called hieroglyphs. Some hieroglyphs were made up of a main picture with elements added to it. These pictures allowed the Maya to express all their ideas. We know about the Aztec culture from their picture writing that still exists today and which is easier to interpret than that of the Maya (Aztec, Inca and Maya, 1993).

2. In contrast to the Mayan pictographs on the following page, the Aztec glyphs are phonetic derivations. "Toch(tli)" means rabbit and "pan(tli)" means banner. "Tul(li) means reed, "(t)lan" means place of, "tzin(tli)" means human posterior, diminutive. "Icpa-c" means on top of and "tape(tl)" means hill.

3. Introduce the Hieroglyph Writing Activity. Have the students choose a partner with whom to write a short story. When it is complete, the partners create pictures (hieroglyphs) that illustrate the words or ideas in the story. Sample glyphs are included on page 172. Have them practice on drawing paper. When the "translation" is complete, teams color the glyphs with markers, cut them out, and glue them onto the construction paper to create a codex.

## Assessment:

Evaluate hieroglyphic writing using the project evaluation sheet on pages 178 and 224.

| Mayan Hieroglyphs | Aztec Hieroglyphs |
|---|---|
| | |

**XOC**
"to count"

**TOCHPAN**
"place of the rabbits"

**TUN**
"year"

**TULANZINCO**
"little place of reeds"

**POP**
"mat of plaited rushes"

**ICPATEPEC**
"on top of the hill"

# LESSON TEN

# MAYANS TODAY

## Objectives:

☞ Students will identify factors in the collapse of these civilizations.
☞ Students will recall contributions of these civilizations which are evident today.
☞ Students will view a video entitled: The Mayan: Apocalypse Then.

**Time:** One day, approximately 2 hours

## Materials:

✂ Video The Mayan: Apocalypse Then distributed by Barr Films

## Procedures:

1.  Discuss the collapse of these civilizations by the Spanish conquest as you conclude the unit on these two ancient Mexican civilizations.

    **Overview:** When the Spanish arrived in the Americas, they knew nothing about the Mesoamerican cultures nor did the inhabitants of the Americas have any knowledge of the Spanish. When Cortés entered Mexico in 1519 his troops easily overpowered resistance. Despite being few in number, the Spanish armies, with their horses and cannons, were stronger. Cortés had the added advantage that the Aztecs believed him to be the king and god Queztalcoatl. Within a short time, the world of the Aztecs was destroyed, their temples razed to the ground, and their emperors murdered. The Maya resisted until 1542, when the Spanish established a capital at Merida.

2.  The final discussion centers on present-day the Maya and Aztec influences. This is an open class discussion. After having learned about their culture, ask: how are we similar? Guide students to discuss how these civilizations have influenced us. Be sure to include their contributions to science and astronomy. The discussion could also consider how we might learn from their history, as some historians believe that the Maya abandoned their cities because of overpopulation, war, and misuse of the environment.

3.  Watch the video which ties it all together.

# LESSON ELEVEN

# PASSPORTS AND REVIEW

## Objectives:

☞ Students will review the information provided during the unit.
☞ Students will complete the passport as a form of review.

## Time: One day, approximately 2 to 3 hours

## Materials:

✂ Passport sheets (included on pages 175 and 176) copied as a double-sided sheet which can be folded in half to create the four page "passport"
✂ Maya and Aztec Project Evaluation Sheet (included on page 178)

## Procedures:

1. Distribute passport sheets (one, double-sided page per student).

2. Have the students complete the passport as a way to help them organize and review the information learned. The teacher can decide to have the students work alone, in pairs, or in small groups.

## Assessment:

Evaluate passport entries using the project evaluation sheet included on pages 178 and 224.

PICTURE OF A PLACE
IN THE CIVILIZATION

NAME OF ANCIENT
CIVILIZATION:

DATE OF VISIT:

CHARACTERISTICS
OF THE CIVILIZATION

TYPE OF RELIGION:

SOCIAL ORGANIZATION:

VISIT COMPLETED ON:

FOOD SOURCES:

GRADE: _____

HOMEWORK POINTS: _____

Page 4

Page 1

| TYPE OF GOVERNMENT: | OBSERVATION NOTES (SUMMARY) |
|---|---|
| SOURCES OF ENTERTAINMENT: | |
| PEOPLE I MET : (CHARACTERS OR LEADERS) | |
| THIS CIVILIZATION'S INFLUENCES ON MY LIFE TODAY: | |
| Page 2 | Page 3 |

# LESSON TWELVE

# ASSESSMENT OF STUDENT LEARNING

## Objectives:

☛ To assess each daily project's quality, completeness, and evidence of understanding of these ancient Mexican civilizations. (Performance Assessment)

☛ To assess students' knowledge of what makes these civilizations true civilizations by identifying the five basic characteristics that distinguish them: their stable food supply, specialization of labor, system of government, social levels, and a highly developed culture that includes art, architecture, religion, music, and law. (Essay Assessment)

☛ To assess students' appreciation for these ancient Mexican civilizations by having them discuss their favorite part of this unit. (Essay Assessment)

**Time:** Two days, approximately 4 to 6 hours

## Materials:

✄ Maya and Aztec Project Evaluation Sheet (included on pages 178 and 224)
✄ Maya and Aztec Essay Quiz (included on pages 179 and 225)

## Procedures:

1. As the teacher had discussed the objectives of the assessments at the start of the unit, review those objectives now while distributing the completed Project Evaluation Sheet. The teacher may wish to have teammates complete an evaluation sheet on each other and have the students complete a self-evaluation. The scores can then be averaged for a final grade.

2. Distribute the Essay Quiz. Read and discuss the questions, and review the criteria for evaluation. The teacher decides whether to use the essay questions as an in-class assignment or as a take-home examination.

Name: ——————————

# Maya and Aztec Project Evaluation Sheet

Each project is rated on a scale from 1 to 4 on the basis of the following criteria:

4 = Product displays top quality work which is complete and demonstrates thorough understanding of the aspect highlighted.

3 = Product displays above average work which is complete and/or demonstrates good understanding of the aspect highlighted.

2 = Product displays average quality work which is slightly incomplete and/or demonstrates an incomplete understanding of the aspect highlighted.

1 = Product displays poor quality work which is incomplete and/or demonstrates a lack of understanding of the aspect highlighted.

1. **Timeline**                                       4   3   2   1

2. **Pyramid silhouette**                      4   3   2   1

3. **Mural scene and facts**                 4   3   2   1

4. **Independent writing activity**      4   3   2   1
     (Personal legend)

5. **Warrior headdress**                      4   3   2   1

6. **Mosaic mask**                                4   3   2   1

7. **Mayan Dance of the Reeds**        4   3   2   1

8. **Patolli game**                                 4   3   2   1
     (Group is evaluated together)

9. **Hieroglyph writing activity**        4   3   2   1

10. **Passport entries**                        4   3   2   1

**Total Points**         ——————————

Name: _____

# Maya and Aztec Essay Quiz

**1. The Maya and the Aztec were true civilizations. Explain the five basic characteristics which distinguished them as civilizations: their stable food supply, specialization of labor, system of government, social levels, and a highly developed culture that included art, architecture, religion, music and law.**

Responses will be rated on a scale from 1 to 4 on the basis of the following criteria:

4 = Response develops all five characteristics in an organized and thorough way.

3 = Response mentions at least four of the five characteristics and/or may be somewhat disorganized or slightly incomplete.

2 = Response mentions only three of the five characteristics and/or may be disorganized or incomplete.

1 = Response mentions only one or two of the five characteristics in a disorganized and incomplete manner.

**2. Discuss your favorite part or parts of this unit. Give details of the projects you completed, why you liked them, and what you learned from them.**

Responses will be rated on a scale from 1 to 4 on the basis of the following criteria:

4 = Response is descriptive, complete, and thoroughly explains the rationale for why the project was liked and what was learned from it.

3 = Response is occasionally descriptive, somewhat complete, and/or basically explains the rationale for why the project was liked and what was learned from it.

2 = Response lacks description, is incomplete, and/or only superficially explains the rationale for why the project was liked and what was learned from it.

1 = Response is not descriptive, is incomplete, and/or does not explain the rationale for why the project was liked and what was learned from it.

## Summary and Suggestions

Unfortunately, as the school year came to an end, there just wasn't enough time for this unit to be implemented. If I were to have had this unit at the beginning of the year, I think I would have chosen to teach it in late April so it could be compared and contrasted to the civilization of Egypt and then followed by the studies of Greece and Rome.

I feel this is a very complete look at the Maya and Aztec. In fact, it might be a little too complete and too involved. I think it takes a full-fledged teaching of the unit to see what works and what doesn't, and if the time has been adequate. It's hard to know what could be taken out, if anything at all. For an evaluation of the unit, one might want to use the essay assessment in which each student writes what project was liked the most. If one or more projects go without mention, then it or they could be left out the following year. I don't think that any of the information should be cut out. If anything it should be expanded, broadened, and deepened. It is important for students to be exposed to the full and complete story. However, the enrichment activities are intended to enhance the unit. If students are not getting out of them what was hoped, these can be eliminated or refined.

## Personal Profile

"You'd make an excellent teacher..." " Education has been wonderful to both of us..." "Teaching is the perfect job for someone who wants to raise kids..." These were the words of encouragement and advice that were given to me by my parents over and over again while I was growing up. Both of my parents spent all of their adult careers in education -- my mother as a teacher and my father as a teacher, counselor, principal, and assistant superintendent. These words of wisdom were repeated so much to me that it seemed like I was listening to a broken record. In fact, at one point I turned away from ever wanting to be a teacher. Now when people ask me what made me finally decide that it was what I wanted to do, I still don't know what changed my mind. I think that everything my parents said made and seemed right all along, but as a teenager and young adult I just didn't want to admit it. Today I am so grateful for my parents' influence on my life. Teaching truly is the perfect occupation for me.

Now I am beginning my sixth year of teaching. I have already moved around from three school sites and have switched grade levels -- from sixth grade to kindergarten. It was while teaching at a predominantly Hispanic middle school that my interest in multicultural education developed. I saw that many of my students lacked a connection to school. This frustrated and intrigued me at the same time. It was during this same period that I began my Master's Degree, which included several courses in multicultural education. I believe it was through these courses that I gained an understanding of my Hispanic students and an awareness of better teaching strategies to meet their needs and interests. It was from this "new-gained" empathy and knowledge that my unit on ancient Mexican civilizations evolved.

# CHAPTER EIGHT

# Multicultural literary guide: A teacher's companion to independent reading in the early elementary grades

## By Doug West

I developed this unit because there were limited guidelines available to determine and define what literature is appropriate to meet the needs of a multicultural classroom. Even though we read and hear about schools and classrooms leaning toward a multicultural approach, it is still new to many educators. Teachers with all good intentions adopt a "tourist approach" to curriculum that appears to be multicultural but simply scrapes the surface. This inspired me to establish sound guidelines that teachers, like myself who are new to the field, can use to search for the type of literature that will fit into a multicultural curriculum.

In my guide to multicultural literature, I focused on the early elementary grade levels because children at these young ages are forming their prejudices, biases, and stereotypes. Dealing with cultural diversity has been a problem throughout United States history, as evidenced by the number of conflicts related to cultural differences. Today, the acceptance of cultural diversity is still a challenge.

One road toward an accepting attitude toward cultural differences may be found in children's literature. Because our values are formed at an early age, it is essential that children be exposed to good literature that celebrates diversity and helps to alleviate the intolerance, prejudice, and injustice suffered by many ethnic groups. Children's literature that focuses on cultural differences and communicates important values of acceptance and tolerance can be very effective. Therefore, the books included here help communicate to children, that all children, no matter what their ethnic backgrounds, have much in common and much to share with others (Gillespie & Rasinski, 1992).

Good literature can also support children between the ages of five and eight years old as they develop interests in the characteristics of culture, start integrating biological and cultural factors, and begin to define a racial and national identity for themselves. Consequently, they have three needs. In the first place, there is a need for children to deepen their sense of pride, to be valued, and to feel appreciated. Secondly, they have a need to build a repertoire of accurate information about themselves and others. Thirdly, children need to determine what is authentic and what is not authentic in cultural representations. Literature can play a role in helping children to recognize stereotyping, develop an emerging sense of fairness, and view racism as neither inevitable nor integral to human nature.

For this literary guide, I define "multicultural children's literature" as literature that represents any distinct cultural group through accurate portrayal and rich detail. In addition, there are three critical elements to get below the surface of multicultural children's literature:  defining "cultural group," the need for "culturally conscious" literature, and the importance of an "inside perspective."

# Defining Cultural Group

A problem in defining "cultural group" is that many times cultures are linked to cultural conglomerates with an umbrella label such as Asian Americans or Native Americans.  Differences are significant among many cultures within each cultural conglomerate.  For example, there are major differences between the Japanese and Korean cultures that fall under the "Asian American" umbrella.

Another problem in defining cultural group is that of excluding some cultures.  For instance, Jewish people feel themselves to be a distinct cultural group but in discussions of multicultural literature, they are usually not included.  Similarly, the exclusion of European Americans in discussions of multicultural literature denies representations of many distinct cultures.  For instance, Patricia Polacco's books about her Jewish Ukrainian cultural heritage meet the criteria for good multicultural literature but are not typically included.

# Culturally Conscious, Culturally Accurate Literature

Culturally conscious books provide exceptional aesthetic experiences.  They entertain, educate, and inform; and they engender racial pride.  This is because these types of books present cultural experiences in a culturally and historically authentic way.  An example of a book meeting these characteristics is Toshi Maruki's Hiroshima No Pika (The Flash of Hiroshima) that portrays the tragedy of the atom bomb that was dropped on Japan in 1945.  The rich details are historically and culturally accurate; also, the story meets the criteria for good literature.

Cultural accuracy means that issues are represented in ways that reflect the values and beliefs of the culture.  For example, Hoang Anh: A Vietnamese American Boy by Diane Hoyt-Goldsmith depicts a Vietnamese American family by showing actual family photographs which portray the family's culture.  Also included in the cultural accuracy definition is richness of details, authentic dialogue and relationships, in-depth treatment of cultural issues, and the inclusion of members of "minority" groups for a purpose.

# Inside Perspective

An inside perspective is one that portrays a cultural group from the point of view of one who is a member of the group.  As a result, the literature represents an authentic view of what the members of the cultural group believe to be true of themselves.  Moreover, by living within a culture, there is a better understanding of the distinctive cultural nuances that are involved.  E-Yen-Shure's (Blue Corn's) I Am a Pueblo Indian Girl reflects her experiences of growing up in a small Indian village. Because this book is based on first-hand experience, the culture is portrayed authentically.

On the other hand, there are authors who successfully write of another cultural group's experiences with a sensitivity acquired through extensive research and participation in cultural groups outside their own. For example, Arnold Adoff is known for his culturally accurate portrayal of African American experiences in books such as Black Is Brown Is Tan even though he was not born of that heritage.

There are many issues that are central to a specific culture. Therefore, it is important to present these issues realistically and explore them indepth so that readers may be able to formulate informed thoughts. For example, segregation in South Africa is the setting for At the Crossroads by Rachel Isadora. The illustrations represent actual scenes that occur in the shanty town families of miner fathers.

## Other Considerations

There are other important issues that need to be considered when selecting multicultural children's literature for the classroom. For instance, rather than overemphasizing historical heritage, it is important to focus on contemporary situations that are portrayed in current lifestyles. In some schools, the curriculum does not relate directly to the child's own life; as a result, this causes the child to be bored with and alienated from school. Books that deal with issues in a child's life help to connect broader social issues with the child's personal experiences (Grant & Sleeter, 1989). Therefore, a balance of various types of books should be included. For example, Eleanor Coerr's Chang's Paper Pony is a story about the son of Chinese immigrants who came to America between 1850 and 1864 during the California Gold Rush. A contemporary link can be made with Murriel Stanek's I Speak English for My Mom, a story of a Mexican American girl who must translate for her mother, who speaks only Spanish. Additionally, a balanced collection should include poetry, biography, nonfiction, and fiction titles which depict a broader spectrum of cultural lives and lifestyles.

Although it is important to recognize the uniqueness of various cultures, there are basic values and experiences that all cultures have in common. For example, Mitsumasa Anno's All in a Day exemplifies both the diversity and the similarities across cultures. Anno's vision for world peace begins with helping children understand the world around them. He accomplishes this by showing how, in a 24-hour period, children all around the world participate in similar kinds of activities such as eating, sleeping, playing, and celebrating the New Year. Books such as this can help children understand the world around them in a much broader scope (Yokota, 1993).

The following pages contain annotated bibliographies and activity ideas for four "cultural conglomerates:" African Americans, Asian Americans, Native Americans, and Latino Americans. I have attempted to diversify those collections as much as possible. However, the bibliographies are not exhaustive. Teachers should expand each section as appropriate to individual classrooms, local resources, and the ever-expanding market for high-quality multicultural children's literature.

# COLLECTION ONE

# AFRICAN AMERICANS

After years of neglect, children's books about African Americans are appearing in greater numbers in both fiction and nonfiction. Several publishers have initiated series that focus on African Americans who have made significant contributions to politics and society. This is because many noteworthy achievers such as the scientist Benjamin Banneker and the explorer Matthew Henson were omitted from textbooks until recently. Recent histories have dealt with resistance to slavery, the civil rights movement, and the role African Americans played in the development of our nation's culture and arts (Miller-Lachmann, 1992). In addition to a selection of fiction and nonfiction titles, the following list of books also includes noteworthy African American achievers who made significant contributions to American society.

**Title:** Amazing Grace
**Author:** Mary Hoffman
**Subject:** Identity, theater

> This book is about a young African American girl named Grace. She loves stories in books and movies or the ones told by her grandmother. Grace acts out the most exciting parts from various stories such as Hiawatha, Aladdin, and Joan of Arc. So when there's the chance to play a part in "Peter Pan," Grace knows exactly who she wants to be. It's hard when her classmates are doubtful, but Grace has the loving support of her mother and wise grandmother to bolster her independence. Grace keeps in mind that she can be anything she wants to be, and the results are amazing.

## Activities:

The twenty-six minute film All Successful People Have It fits into the theme expressed in Amazing Grace: a person can be anything she or he wants to be. This will give young children inspiration to set high goals for themselves by seeing what qualitites successful people have in common, regardless of their race or economic background. It discusses the importance of setting a goal, inspiring the desire for it, and showing how to develop a plan for accomplishment.

**Title:** Ashanti to Zulu: African Traditions
**Author:** Margaret Musgrove
**Subject:** African tribes

This stunning picture book describes the cultures of twenty-six African tribes from the Ashanti to the Zulu. The author accurately relates ceremonies, celebrations, and day-to-day customs. In order to show as much about the different tribes as possible, the beautiful illustrations include a man, a woman, a child, their living quarters, an artifact, and a local animal.

## Activities:

The nineteen minute video Africa: History and Culture examines the history and influences that shaped the development of Africa's cultures. To contrast Africa's history with contemporary Africa, the twenty-seven minute video Africa: A New Look focuses on contemporary Africans. It shows primary schools and universities, family farms, religious services, health clinics, businesses, a TV studio, and political rallies, with a sequence on South Africa and its racial policy.

**Title:** At the Crossroads
**Author:** Rachel Isadora
**Subject:** Segregation, South Africa

Rachel Isadora has made numerous trips to South Africa. The illustrations represent actual scenes that take place in one of many shanty towns in South Africa. These towns spring up to house the families of the fathers who work far from their homes. At the crossroads, the children are singing and dancing. Their fathers are coming home. This is not an unusual scene in the segregated townships of South Africa where the fathers who work in the mines are far away for many months at a time, and their families are not permitted to join them.

## Activities:

A discussion with the children on the unfairness of discrimination and prejudice would be appropriate at this time; also, the unfair treatment of hardworking people who receive very low wages in order for others to profit from their labor. Afterwards, the twenty-five minute film South Africa Today will be excellent to show because the children will connect what they are learning in the classroom to reality in the real world.

**Title:** Bigmama's
**Author:** Donald Crews
**Subject:** Family

The author, Donald Crews, and his sisters grew up in Newark, New Jersey. As a boy, he and his family spent their summer vacations in Cottondale,

Florida, where his grandparents lived on a country farm.  Their grandmother was called Bigmama not because she was big but because she was their Mama's Mama.  This book shows the African American love of family togetherness that the author still cherishes today as a grownup with a family of his own.  The illustrations show Bigmama's farm with an outhouse, a well, chickens, and other things of "real life way out in the country."  Also included is a black and white photograph that shows Donald and his sisters fishing on Bigmama's lake during their childhood.

## Activities:

The eight minute video Families illustrates nuclear and extended families, family members' roles, support families provide, and community members who participate in helping children grow up.  After seeing this video, the teacher can guide children to share personal experiences: trips to visit grandparents, community helpers who have influenced their lives, and other themes of the book and the video.

## Title: Black Is Brown Is Tan
## Author: Arnold Adoff
## Subject: Race awareness

This poetic book sends a message to children that there are different races and this is the way we are: "Black is brown is tan is girl is boy is nose to face is all the colors of the race."  Colorful illustrations show the life of an African American family: barbecuing outdoors, laughing with one another, and enjoying each other.  Nobody is ashamed or considers color of skin a major issue because this is the way people are throughout the world.

## Activities:

The seventy-five minute video entitled Many Voices I  has five segments: What's in a Name, To Jew Is Not a Verb, Quick to Judge, Food for Thought, and Hair Scare. Each of these fifteen minute segments explores stereotyping, discrimination, and racism from a child's point of view, and each one focuses on a child trying to come to terms with his or her background.  After the children see a program, the teacher can ask the children to answer verbally or in writing this question, "How am I different as a result of this lesson?" (Lazear, 1994).

## Title: Harriet Tubman and Black History Month
## Author: Polly Carter
## Subject: Biography

This biography of Harriet Tubman is written for beginning readers and older youngsters who have difficulty reading. Each of the four chapters is only a few pages long so the text is simple, yet exciting. Dialogue is taken from Harriet Tubman's own words. The incidents recounted in this short biography are accurate and involve feelings that young children can understand (Miller-Lachmann, 1992).

## Activities:

The biography of Harriet Tubman is an excellent way to start a discussion focusing on African American women. The sixty minute program series entitled Many Voices II consists of four fifteen minute films: A Sari Tale, Mother Tongue, The World at My Door, and Positively Native. These films explore stereotyping, discrimination, and racism from a child's point of view. These films may serve as a good lead-in to discussions about why it is important for children to practice citizenship in their community and to become change agents in order to establish equality, as did Harriet Tubman.

**Title:** Jackie Robinson: He Was the First
**Author:** David A. Adler
**Subject:** Racism, baseball

Though legitimate role models for young boys are too often situated in the world of sports (to the exclusion of other professions), this biography is well done. The story, like Tubman's, is one of combating racism. However, what sets this book apart from others is Adler's sensitivity. He conveys the racism of the time without repeating racial slurs and epithets (Miller-Lachmann, 1992).

## Activities:

The video series Baseball Classics contains four volumes about famous baseball players. The section about Jackie Robinson is excellent because it shows his courage to keep on playing baseball despite negative criticism. There are actual testimonies from players, his wife, and baseball commentators that tell about the hardships Robinson overcame.

**Title:** Martin Luther King
**Author:** Linda Lowery
**Subject:** Civil rights, unjust laws

The book begins with an author's note in which terms such as "civil rights" and "unjust laws" are explained. The text covers the highlights of King's life and the civil rights era (Miller-Lachmann, 1992). Too often a study of Martin Luthor King's life is confined to the federal holiday which honors him or to Black History month. This book can be used in the context of sharing the genre of biographies with children or simply made available to them as a natural part of a classroom which values diversity, rather than compartmentalizing it.

## Activities

The Boyhood of Martin Luther King, Jr. which is thirteen minutes long. This video contains actual incidents from King's boyhood and traces the influences that shaped his life. Keep in mind that omitting the mention of other African Americans such as Bishop Turner may perpetuate the misconception that African American leaders other than King did not exist. To maintain an accurate perspective, it would be appropriate to show the nine minute video Bishop Turner, among others. This tells about his life as an African American leader and how he influenced the Civil Rights movement with his ideas.

**Title:** Tell Me a Story, Mama
**Author:** Angela Johnson
**Subject:** Family, values

As a mother puts her daughter to bed, the little girl listens to stories about her mother's childhood. This is a childhood memoir of a mother as told by her little girl. The child has heard the stories so many times that she can recite them almost by heart. The stories place her at the center of an intergenerational family. Nurturing values learned in one era are passed along to each succeeding generation. Aid in times of need comes not only from one's immediate family but also from grandparents, aunts, and uncles. The interdependence of this extended African American family makes this an ideal picture book for showing to children in the primary grades (Miller-Lachmann, 1992).

## Activities:

The ninety minute film series Getting to Know Me has three thirty minutes segments: Momma Violet's Arrival, The Naming of Kwane, and The Wish. These are stories of a southern African American family's heritage that are passed down through generations, give real meaning to the culture, and preserve the family values for future generations. After showing the film, the class can start a unit on family history. The children can start inquiring about their roots by asking their parents and relatives what they know of their ancestors and if any photographs are available. Another important point to make to the children is that we can learn a lot from other cultures that we can apply to our own lives, such as the appreciation that African Americans have for their ancestors.

**Title:** What a Morning! The Christmas Story in Black Spirituals
**Author:** John M. Langstaff
**Subject:** Music: voice, piano

This book gives a visual rendition of Negro spirituals selected to tell the Christmas story. The idea of a children's book featuring an African American holy family is a unique idea and a welcome one. Langstaff selected five spirituals and the arrangements for voice and piano are on two-page spreads. Opposite the music is a one-page picture. Each song is introduced by a corresponding biblical verse. Now whether or not this holiday book is appropriate in public school is open to debate because religious material can be perceived as inappropriate. So as a teacher, be careful (Miller-Lachmann, 1992).

## Activities:

The twenty minute video <u>Discovering the Music of Africa</u> is excellent to show since it connects to music in the African American heritage. It shows basic instruments from Ghana such as drums, bells, and rattles; also, it demonstrates the use of rhythms, dances, and communication. One can complement the unit by presenting biographies of famous musicians, investigating different contemporary musical instruments derived from basic instruments, and tracing the development of musical genres; such as jazz, blues, and rock.

**COLLECTION TWO**

**ASIAN AMERICANS**

Asian Americans are the fastest growing and most diverse minority group in the United States. The number of Asian Americans grew from 3.8 million in 1980 to 6.9 million in 1989. This eighty percent increase was spurred by 2.4 million Asian immigrants who arrived in the United States during the 1980's. Among the leading countries of origin are the Philippines, Vietnam, China, Korea, Taiwan, Cambodia, India, Laos, and Japan. By the year 2010, as much as thirty-eight percent of Americans under the age eighteen will belong to minority groups. Therefore it is incumbent upon us and our children to learn more about the cultures of these newest Americans (Miller-Lachmann, 1992).

**Title:** <u>The Bracelet</u>
**Author:** Yoshiko Uchida
**Subject:** Japanese internment

> This is a work of historical fiction. It is about the evacuation of people of Japanese ancestry from the West Coast during World War II, as seen through the eyes of a second grader. Japanese American, Emi, watches the family possessions being carted away, misses her father who was sent to a prison

camp, and feels the loss and dislocation of a situation that she cannot understand. Emi, her mother, and her sister, Reiko, are about to leave for the train station taking only what they can carry with them when Emi's friend, Laurie Madison, comes with a present. Laurie gives Emi a bracelet to remember her by. Somewhere during the journey from Berkeley to the racetrack where they are housed in a horse stall, Emi loses the bracelet. At first she is devastated, but eventually she realizes that Laurie's gift of friendship and reassurance will stay with her no matter what happens (Heilbig & Perkins, 1994).

## Activities:

Discuss with the children what effect the camps had on Japanese American family life. Describe how you would feel about being forced to leave your home. Laurie gave Emi a bracelet before she left on the train. What did this symbolize? (Carnes, 1995). Teaching Tolerance, a publication of the Southern Poverty Law Center, has back issues available which focus on the internment of Japanese Americans. They contain some excellent ideas for teaching this difficult issue from our national history. Consider sharing other stories about Japanese Americans with the children, such as How My Parents Learned to Eat.

**Title:** Grandfather's Dream
**Author:** Holly Keller
**Subject:** Ecology

The war in Vietnam was over, but the cranes that had once covered the sky still did not return. It was Grandfather's dream, which young Nam shared, that the dikes would cause the land to be flooded so that the plants would grow and the cranes would return. This story of a dream that comes true is more than a story of a family, it is a story of commitment to continuity and to the future. Young Nam reminds us that we all must share and inherit Grandfather's dream if the creatures of the world are to have a safe place to live. The illustrations are accurate, showing typical villages in Vietnam including the main foods that the Vietnamese eat: rice, fish, and pork. We also see the land outlined with rice paddies nourished by the monsoon rains, the simple houses built with bamboo and grass, and the water buffalo that are common throughout the country. All of these give authenticity of meaning to the story.

## Activities:

The pictures accurately portray the rural environment of the Vietnamese. After the war, thousands of Vietnamese fled to America because of political oppression. As a result, Vietnamese Americans have experienced cultural shock and psychological depression many because our environment contrasts sharply with the simple, close-knit lifestyle of rural Vietnam. It would be very appropriate to show parts of the ninety minute film Pacific Bridges I.

These three thirty minute programs help children understand Asian American migration, stereotyping, economic exploration, and racial oppression.

**Title:** <u>Hoang Anh: A Vietnamese American Boy</u>
**Author:** Diane Hoyt-Goldsmith
**Subject:** Vietnamese Americans

Hoang Anh arrived in the United States as a baby when his family escaped from Vietnam in a fishing boat. Describing his new life in America, Hoang Anh tells about his home and school. Like other kids his age, Hoang Anh rides a bike, plays football, listens to popular music, eats pizza, and enjoys video games. But also he participates in the customs and rituals that his family brought from Vietnam. He eats traditional food at mealtimes and speaks Vietnamese at home. This book contains actual photographs of the daily life of Hoang Anh and his family, including ones taken in Vietnam before the family came to America. The book truly reflects the lifestyle, native culture, and traditions of a refugee Vietnamese family in contemporary America.

## Activities:

The twenty-six minute video <u>Overture: Link From Vietnam</u> is about the life of a young Vietnamese girl, Linh Tran, and her family in their first real home since emigrating from Vietnam. Linh and Jose Aguilar, a neighbor, become friends after discovering mutual interests in playing the flute. Afterwards, the teacher can lead a discussion with the children on the importance of making friendships with newcomers so that they will not be alienated from others and experience loneliness.

**Title:** <u>I Hate English</u>
**Author:** Ellen Levine
**Subject:** Identity, adjustment

This book details the experiences of a young Chinese girl, Mei Mei, and her family's move to New York's Chinatown. Mei is comfortable with people like herself but, when faced with the challenges of a schoolroom, Mei Mei refuses to speak the strange new English language. An astute teacher eventually breaks down the barrier Mei Mei has placed between herself and the new society in which she lives. The book deals realistically and sympathetically with the issues of cultural differences as Mei Mei adjusts to a new society while desperately trying to hold on to her old life and its traditions.

## Activities:

Class discussions should focus on how Mei Mei reacts to the changes in her life. Children can keep journals on their feelings about the differences of cultures around them. Can children detect cultural differences in their everyday lives? Explore with the children different strategies for welcoming new children into the classroom. Try to elicit from children statements of empathy for new children. List these strategies and post them in the classroom (Gillespie & Rasinski, 1992).

**Title:** Kimako's Story
**Author:** June Jordan
**Subject:** Alienation

Seven year old Kimako lives with her mother and baby brother in an inner-city neighborhood in New York. When her mother goes back to work at the beginning of the summer, Kimako is left alone to take care of her brother. This is a culturally conscious book that portrays urban life in realistic detail even though it is from a child's point of view. The language is very simple, yet it evokes the sights, sounds, and dangers that occur in an urban area. Kimako's acceptance of herself, adaptability, and resourcefulness, as evidenced by her reliance upon reading rather than TV to fill the emptiness in her life, her creation of the puzzle poems, and her use of a neighbor's dog, are the keys to her own survival and an inspiration to young children of all races (Miller-Lachmann, 1992).

### Activities:

The forty-six minute video Coming Across tells about the millions of immigrants living in America. They come from Central America, Southeast Asia, Mexico, Iran, and Russia in search of a better life. Five native born American teens step into the lives of immigrant families from ten countries to share their experiences. This video will connect to the multicultural environment depicted in Kimako's Story.

**Title:** Sadako and the Thousand Paper Cranes
**Author:** Eleanor Corn
**Subject:** Death

This book is based on the life of a real little girl, Sadako Sasaki, who lived in Japan from 1943 to 1955. She was in Hiroshima when the atom bomb was dropped in 1945. Ten years later she died as a result of the radiation from the bomb; therefore, Sadako's courage made her a heroine to children in Japan. When she died on October 25, 1955, her classmates folded 356 cranes so that a total of 1,000 would be buried with her. Afterwards, the young people throughout Japan helped collect money to have a monument built to honor her and all the children killed by the atom bomb. In 1958, a statue was unveiled in Hiroshima Peace Park showing Sadako standing on top of a granite mountain of paradise holding a golden crane in outstretched hands. The theme of the book is the children's wish engraved on the base of the statue: "This is our cry; This is our prayer; peace in the world."

## Activities:

The expression that the Japanese children displayed to Sadako is an expression of love which is universal throughout the world. Therefore an excellent ten minute film to show is <u>Love's Beginning</u> which shows the universal need for love which grows into a universal reciprocity such as the love that Sadako received.

**Title:** <u>Tall Boy's Journey</u>
**Author:** Joanna Halpert Kraus
**Subject:** Relocation, adjustment

This is a realistic novela of a present day Korean village boy's adjustment to life in the United States. After his grandmother dies, over the boy's protest, his soldier uncle puts orphan Kim Moo Yong, about eight, on a plane for the United States, telling him to "be tall, inside." Adopted by an American scientist and his wife, the boy is determined to return to Korea. He tries to run away, refuses food, and generally proves to be difficult. Eventually his American father's colleague, Mr. Cho, becomes his mentor, explains American ways to him, encourages him to make friends, and urges him to take advantage of this opportunity for a good life. The book, an almost clinical account of adjustment, introduces young readers to the trauma of relocation and what might be expected if a family adopts such an orphan. This story is based on the experiences of the author's own adopted son and other children like him (Heilbig & Perkins, 1994).

## Activities:

The twenty-four minute film <u>Korea</u> shows Korea as a land divided by war but cemented by tradition. It follows Yung Je, a twelve year old girl, as she prepares to become a Cheju Island diver like her mother was and shows the traditional roles that the Korean culture dictates to women. This film is a good way to explain Kim's uncle's role as a soldier and Kim's difficult adjustment to American life because of his strong cultural ties to Korea.

# COLLECTION THREE

# NATIVE AMERICANS

Anthropologists believe that Native American peoples migrated to the Americas as long as thirty to sixty thousand years ago, during the ice ages that created the land bridge from Asia to the Americas. Very little information is available for young people on the earliest history of Native American peoples; therefore, many nonfiction books on Native Americans briefly allude to the theories of the migration of these early peoples. The books listed will give young children historical, cultural, and contemporary information on several Native American groups (Miller-Lachmann, 1992).

**Title:** Alice Yazzie's Year
**Author:** Ramona Maher
**Subject:** Navajo

> In January, Yas Nilt'ees, "snow covered the world." The day is cold and still; the smoke rises straight up from the chimney. The sound of the horses pawing the snow for graze carries a long way. Their breath is white smoke, frosting their noses. All these things are apparent from the breath-taking illustrations. When the strip-mining machines tear up the earth, the shattering roar of their destruction is nearly audible. There is not a page of this book that is not beautiful. Alice and her grandfather are so real that you would think that they are your friends. In addition, there is an afterword by the author, "Notes About the Navajo Country and Ways of Life," that completes the book (Stapin & Seale, 1989).

**Activities:**

> The fourteen minute video Indian Crafts: Hopi, Navajo, and Iroquois connects to the Navajo culture of Alice and her grandfather as well as learning about the Hopi and Iroquois cultures. This film shows basket making, pottery making, kachina carving, weaving, jewelry making and mask carving as developed by these tribes. The illustrations show the wide range of arts practiced by the Indians which enriches the art of the United States.

**Title:** Buffalo Woman
**Author:** Paul Goble
**Subject:** Plains Nations

> A folktale like this is common to all cultures. That is, the hero is given a supernatural wife but loses her through some fault of his own or through the malice of others. In this case, a "great hunter" who has always been respectful to the buffalo is rewarded with a beautiful wife. They have a son, Buffalo Calf, but the hunter's relatives are unkind, and on a day when the hunter is away, the Buffalo Woman takes the boy and leaves the camp. The hunter follows, but he must face danger and pick his wife and son out of the herd. This he does, with the help of his supernatural son, and he is then transformed by the Buffalo Nation into "a young buffalo bull." Goble treats the material with great respect accompanied by lovely illustrations (Stapin & Seale, 1989).

## Activities:

The buffalo is highly respected by the Indians because the animals were their source of food and the hides were used for clothing. To connect the buffalo with an activity, the fifteen minute film Indian Family of Long Ago reenacts the life of the Sioux Indian tribe in South Dakota as a wandering tribe of buffalo hunters. Scenes of camp life, education of the young, and a buffalo hunt are followed by a feast of celebration. The costumes are authentic.

**Title:** I Am a Pueblo Indian Girl
**Author:** E-Yen-Shure (Blue Corn)
**Subject:** Pueblo Indians

This first-person narrative tells how the author grew up in a small Pueblo Indian village. Blue Corn explains her belief in Earth Mother, who provides her tribe with corn, beans, squash, and fruit. Earth is the mother of all things. She describes the wide open beautiful lands of New Mexico and includes a picture of her home. Moreover, illustrations with explanations highlight important aspects of Blue Corn's culture: clothes, ponies, baking bread, and other day-to-day activities. These illustrations are drawn by actual Indian artists--Navajo, Apache, Pueblo.

## Activities:

The twelve minute film Indian Art of the Pueblos is a good follow-up to Blue Corn's narrative as it gives more insight into the Pueblo culture. The film provides an introduction to the native arts and crafts of the Pueblo Indians, and it examines the significance of these works in the religious and social life of the tribes. It acquaints children with the works of several contemporary Pueblo artists and artisans.

**Title:** Tohono O'odham: Lives of the Desert People
**Authors:** Tohono O'odham Tribal Council
**Subject:** Tohono O'odham/Papago

Tohono O'odham are the people commonly referred to as Papago. This book begins with the Creation Story. Land, farming, gathering, hunting, dress and lifestyles are discussed. Both past and present are considered. One really nice thing is the songs that are included: songs for hunting, for success in a race, songs for singing up the corn, and a lullaby. A song is an integral part of all Native ceremonials and the context is given.

## Activities:

The fifteen minute video Desert Regions: Nomads and Traders shows how the Navajo Indians of Monument Valley and the Bedouins of Jordan have learned to survive in the desert. This film will show that their survival is a beautiful relationship with Mother Earth even though the desert is a harsh environment.

**Title:** The Mishomis Book:  The Voice of the Ojibway
**Author:** Edward Benton-Benai
**Subject:** Ojibway

The author is the Executive Director of The Red School House in St. Paul, MN, and a member of the Fish Clan of the Ojibway Nation.  He has a concern for the negative and inaccurate ways in which Native Americans' lives are portrayed in America.  Therefore, Benton-Benai offers us the teachings of his people.   Mishomis begins with the Creation Story and tells how Original Man came to be on the Earth, how he learned his name, how he found his Grandmother, how he searched the Earth for his Mother and Father, and how, as Waynaboozhoo, he became a hero and a teacher for the Ojibway People.   As a child must be guided to grow in understanding, so does Mishomis take the reader from the simplest beginnings to the complexity of meaning in the Midewiwin and Sweat Lodge Ceremonies.  This book totally confounds the usual Indian stereotypes and it is highly recommended to introduce children in the mainstream culture to a more realistic and truthful manner about the lives and cultures of the tribal peoples of America.  It is hard to imagine that anyone could read this and not come away from it at least a little more open to the beauty and strangeness of life (Stapin & Seale, 1989).

## Activities

The appreciation for Native American culture that The Mishomis Book gives to our children is a good connection to the twenty-two minute video Indians in the Americas.  It discusses how the Indians came to the Americas, how and where they settled, their culture, and their contributions to modern-day society.  Before viewing the video, create a 3-step chart with the class which lists what they know about Native Americans and what questions they have.  After the video, ask the children what they have learned and compare their charts.

**Title:** Our Voices, Our Land
**Authors:** Harvey Lloyd and Stephen Trimble
**Subject:** Southwestern Nations

This book portrays the Native peoples of the Southwest.  The entire text is in the words of Native people who live in this part of the country and that is what makes this book so good to use with children.  One word of caution: Our Voice, Our Land would be an easy book to misuse.  Be careful not to romanticize the people who are speaking.  There is something to be learned here if you allow yourself to listen to what they are saying (Stapin & Seale, 1989).

## Activities:

The nineteen minute video <u>Indian Boy of the Southwest</u> is a good connection to <u>Our Voice, Our Land</u> because it bears witness to the lives and lifestyle of a Hopi Indian family living in the Arizona desert. The video shows an understanding of how they are able to sustain a full and happy life among such seemingly harsh conditions.

**Title:** <u>A Promise Is a Promise</u>
**Authors:** Michael Kusugal and Robert Munsch
**Subject:** Eskimos

<u>A Promise Is a Promise</u> is a delightful blend of the modern and traditional Eskimo cultures. Allashua lives in an ordinary house; she has her books and her teddy bear. This is a whimsical story of a wonderfully warm and loving family.

## Activities:

This book can lead into the seventeen minute film <u>Eskimos: A Changing Culture</u> that portrays the lifestyle of the Eskimos living near the Bering Sea. It details the extent of changes in family patterns, values, and other elements of Eskimo culture due to modern technology.

**Title:** <u>The People Shall Continue</u>
**Author:** Simon J. Ortiz
**Subject:** All nations

This book is a superb overview of a Nation's history. Ortiz is a poet and it shows in his prose. With simplicity, without polemic, Ortiz gives the true story of how it was, how it is, and, with hope and a little luck, maybe how it will come to be, for all of us. Ortiz tells the names of heroes: Pope, Tecumseh, Black Hawk, Crazy Horse, Osceola, Joseph, Sitting Bull, and Captain Jack. He speaks of the constant betrayal, broken treaties, broken promises, and the taking away of children. If you read only one book about Native Americans to young children, let it be this one (Stapin & Seale, 1989).

## Activities:

The eighteen minute video <u>The Indian Experience: After 1500 A. D.</u> shows how the Indians were unwillingly drawn into conflicts so that the United States government could take control of their land after the settling of North America. It covers the causes and effects of the conflicts with the Indians after independence was declared. This video is a good connection to the theme of "the People will continue" in Ortiz's book.

**Title:** Red Ribbons for Emma
**Authors:** New Mexico People and Energy Collective
**Subject:** Navajo

For most Americans, knowledge of conflict between Native peoples and power companies is probably limited to a vague familiarity with the words "Big Mountain." For Emma Yazzie, the conflict is part of everyday life. Emma and the other rural Navajos look different from heroes we usually read about, who are mostly "White men." But she is a hero, and this is her story. When this book was written in 1981, Emma Yazzie had been fighting the power companies for fifteen years. She went to court to stop the plant and the mine, a case she lost. The writing does not romanticize the difficulty and poverty of Emma Yazzie's life; neither does it allow pity. Emma's indomitable spirit and sense of humor demonstrate clearly why we so value our Elders, and why the men say no Nation is defeated, so long as the hearts of the women are strong (Stapin & Seale, 1989).

### Activities:

Show the video <u>Weave of Time: The Story of a Navajo Family 1938-1986.</u> This portrays four generations affected by change enforced by the United States government and the justice system. After the students see the video, ask them how the changes are relevant to Emma Yazzie's life as well as to other Native Americans.

# COLLECTION FOUR

# LATINO AMERICANS

Although the Latino culture is not limited to Mexico, this chapter focuses on Mexico as a priority for California and other Western states. Given Mexico's size and proximity to the United States, it is puzzling that the body of literature about such an important "good neighbor" lacks the depth of coverage it deserves. The currently available children's books about Mexico are aimed primarily at providing young readers with the essential, basic information that any good student is expected to know about a country. What is lacking are books on Mexico that highlight the distinct cultures and cultural groups unique to specific regions or states within the country. Additionally, there is little in the way of fiction that exposes children to the richness of Mexican culture or the beauty of the land (Miller-Lachmann, 1992).

**Title:** <u>The Adventures of Connie and Diego</u>
**Author:** Maria Garcia
**Subject:** Identity

Connie and Diego are twins, born "with many colors" over their little bodies. They looked so funny that their sisters and brothers started to laugh. When the twins are old enough, they run away in search of a place where no one will make fun of them. Eventually, they accept their difference from other people and realize that otherwise they are just like anyone else. Some may be disappointed that the story does not have a fairy-tale ending. But for those born "different," there is seldom a fairy-tale ending (Schon, 1991).

**Activities:**

The nineteen minute film <u>Lee Suzuki: Home in Hawaii</u> is about Lee Suzuki of Hawaiian, Japanese, Filipino, Irish, and Swedish ancestry. The film represents not only the rich racial mixture of Hawaii but a hope for the future that everybody, regardless of different mixtures of ethnicity, can live in harmony. This film makes a good connection to the twins of different colors.

**Title:** <u>Arroz con Leche: Popular Songs and Rhymes From Latin America</u>
**Author:** Lulu Delacre
**Subject:** Rhymes, songs

Twelve well-known nursery rhymes and children's songs from Mexico, Puerto Rico, and Argentina are included in this delightful bilingual collection.

**Activities:**

The twenty-one minute video <u>Discovering the Music in Latin America</u> shows how Latino music is a blend from many cultures, including the Indians and the Spanish. This video is an excellent connection to the songs and rhymes learned in <u>Arroz con Leche</u>.

**Title:** <u>Benito Juarez</u>
**Author:** Jan Gleiter

**Title:** <u>Bernardo de Galvez</u>
**Author:** Frank De Varona

**Title:** <u>Carlos Finlay</u>
**Authors:** Christine Sumption and Kathleen Thompson

**Title:** <u>Luis W. Alvarez</u>
**Author:** Corinn Codye

**Title:** <u>Pedro Menendez de Aviles</u>

**Author:** Kathleen Thompson

**Title:** Queen Isabella the First
**Author:** Corinn Codye

**Title:** Sor Juana Ines de la Cruz
**Author:** Kathleen Thompson

**Title:** Vilma Martinez
**Author:** Kathleen Thompson

The preceding eight books are a collection of thirty-two page biographies that can be the foundation for a bilingual literature collection of Latinos who made significant contributions. Through reading about the lives of these eight Latino men and women from the United States, Cuba, Spain, and Mexico, young readers will learn about people who were able to make the world a better place.

## Activities:

The twenty-six minute film All Successful People Have It is an excellent connection to these biographies as it examines the importance of establishing goals, inspiring the desire for goals, and developing a plan to accomplish goals. Children can recognize that they, too, have the potential to succeed and to make the world a better place just as the famous persons in these biographies have done.

**Title:** A Family in Mexico
**Author:** Tom Moran
**Subject:** Family

A simple text details the daily life of a nine year old girl living in Oaxaca, Mexico. Children learn basic facts and interesting customs of these people. The text balances photographs of a middle-class family and poor rural scenes (Schon, 1991).

## Activities:

The twelve minute film Market Place in Mexico shows a serape maker, a potter, and a rope maker in a small Mexican village. This film shows how the people are dependent upon one another and how everyone in a community has an important contribution to make.

**Title:** Family Pictures/Cuadros de Familia
**Author:** Carmen Lomas Garza
**Subject:** Family

This easy-to-read, bilingual (English/Spanish) picture book recounts the author's experiences as a young Latino girl in Texas. Fiestas, family gatherings, holidays, religion, and other activities of a closely-knit Mexican-American family ground the text in culture authenticity.

**Activities:**

The seventeen minute film <u>A Mexican American Family</u> will add insights about a Mexican American family. The film depicts the problems, influences, and conditions of life and work for Mexican Americans living in Los Angeles.

**Title:** <u>Hector Lives in the United States Now: The Story of a Mexican American Child</u>
**Author:** Joan Hewett
**Subject:** Contemporary Mexican-American

Through Hector's story, readers are exposed to the daily life of a Mexican American family as well as the two important events in their lives: first communion and legal residency in the United States through the Immigration Reform and Control Act. Black and white photographs of Hector and his family provide a close look at their numerous activities (Schon, 1991).

**Activities:**

The fifteen minute video <u>Lost Is a Feeling</u> is about Amador, who moves from Puerto Rico to Washington, D. C., and tries to meet some playmates. This video helps children to understand how people feel lost and threatened in new situations. Afterwards, the teacher can lead a discussion about how students would feel if they were to move to a different city or country.

**Title:** <u>An Inca Farmer</u>
**Author:** Marion Morrison
**Subject:** Inca Empire

The text describes the life of a farmer in the Inca Empire before the arrival of the Spaniards: daily life, food, crime and punishment, and festivals and gods during Incan times.

**Activities:**

When teaching about other cultures, it is important to give historical background so that children can form a connection between a culture's past and present day (Grant & Sleeter, 1993). Therefore, it would be appropriate at this time to show the eighteen minute video <u>Indian Origins: The First 50,000 Years.</u> This video shows how the first people arrived on the North American continent and where they settled. It also provides evidence from the archaic periods up through the development of pottery.

**Title:** I Speak English for My Mom
**Author:** Muriel Stanek
**Subject:** Contemporary Mexican American

Lupe, a Mexican American girl, translates for her Spanish-speaking mother. They are shown going to the doctor and to the store, talking to Lupe's teacher, and other activities. This is a realistic story about a Mexican American girl and her mother, who work and study hard in their new country. It must be noted that most Latinos in the United States want to learn English, but this is not the key to their existence, as this story implies (Schon, 1991).

## Activities:

The thirty-two minute film Becoming American is a story of Hang Sou and his family, agrarian refugees from the highlands of Laos, who work to make a new life amid the complexities of an American city.

**Title:** The Most Beautiful Place in the World
**Author:** Ann Cameron
**Subject:** Family

The sad realities of poverty in Guatemala are poignantly portrayed in this warm story about a hard working, seven year old boy and his grandmother. Some readers may question Juan's last thought at the end, "where you love somebody a whole lot, and you know that person loves you, that's the most beautiful place in the world." This would be hard to imagine especially when Juan was abandoned by his parents and experienced so much tragedy at such a tender age. Nevertheless, this is an inspiring story that will affect young readers (Schon, 1991).

## Activities:

The ten minute film Love's Beginning shows the universal need for love and love as a powerful force that will help one to overcome life's hardships.

**Title:** My House/ Mi Casa
**Author:** Rebecca Emberley
**Subject:** Spanish language

In simple, bold, and colorful images, Emberley invites the youngest readers to learn basic words in both Spanish and English. This book makes learning a new language fun and is the perfect way to introduce the very young to the richness of our multicultural society.

## Activities:

Spanish is a wonderful language to learn and it can be especially fun when children see the similarities between English and Spanish. Bilingual books, such as this one, should be available to children as a natural extension of their curiosity about language and the "way to say" things. The children will realize that to learn another language is not so difficult once they see the similarities in such a pleasant form.

## Summary and Suggestions

The knowledge that I acquired to write this unit came from Junko Yokota (1993). I used her criteria for evaluating multicultural literature in assessing authors of children's literature. In determining the types of literature that are appropriate for a multicultural approach, I initially struggled to find books that fit Yokota's criteria. I searched in libraries, bookstores, and private collections. The literature that I initially reviewed did not really hit the target (so to speak). However, I persevered and found that libraries contain excellent resources for surveying children's literature. Teachers can find excellent professional resources through their local library; a list is included in the Reference Appendix for this chapter. After reading very good book reviews, I was able to find appropriate books. These detailed reviews increased my confidence that there is quality literature available, and more is being written every day. A good resource for teachers is the Multicultural Review. This monthly periodical reviews much of the new multicultural literature available and provides useful bibliographies of books on selected topics.

Now that I have found an effective method to evaluate children's multicultural literature, I need to find literature for the secondary school level. Older students who are entering adulthood can develop an appreciation for cultural diversity. They need to recognize the hardships, sacrifices, and injustices that different cultures experienced in a country where "equality" was for everyone. Secondary students will soon be in a position to make a positive change in our society and to practice good citizenship by making our democracy a true democracy. By exposing secondary students to high-quality multicultural literature and authors, classroom teachers can meet the challenge of diversity and make a significant contribution to our students and the future of equality and democracy in America.

## Personal Profile

I served in the Marine Corps for twenty three years and I am now making a career transition into the education field. Being in the military, I can honestly say that I was a teacher throughout my whole career. It was my responsibility to train personnel under my supervision so that they would be proficient in their duties and have the confidence to eventually perform their duties with minimal supervision.

My interest in teaching multicultural education is due to my travels in Asia and my rewarding experiences serving with military personnel from diverse cultural backgrounds. As a result, I have a strong desire to share these experiences and the cultural richness that can be gained from having a genuine appreciation for those who make up our diverse society. Moreover, I would very much like for my students to acquire a strong desire to travel so that they can broaden their horizons and be enlightened by other cultures in a way that can be cherished throughout their lives.

At this time I have obtained a Master's Degree in Multicultural Education from United States International University. At the present time I am looking for a substitute/ permanent full-time teaching position. I feel confident in guiding students through a productive and meaningful curriculum that greatly enhances their awareness and appreciation of our diverse multicultural American society.

# ASSESSMENT APPENDIX

## Assessments for Chapter Three:   Celebrations with a twist

## MASK
## PARAGRAPH

Each student will write a paragraph (at least FIVE sentences in length) responding to the following topic:

### "Why People Wear Masks"

Paragraphs will be evaluated based on the following scale:

4   The response provides more than five statements supporting the topic. Sentences are clearly developed and convincing.

3   The response provides at least five statements supporting the topic. The sentences are somewhat clear but not convincing.

2   The response addresses the topic, but is not developed sufficiently.

1   The response fails to address the topic and/or is poorly developed.

Name: _____

## Comedy/Tragedy Quiz

Decide whether each event is comic (C) or tragic (T). Circle the appropriate letter. *A total of 6 points is possible in this section.*

| | | | |
|---|---|---|---|
| 1. | You lose your favorite toy. | C | T |
| 2. | Your best friend moves away. | C | T |
| 3. | You see a funny movie. | C | T |
| 4. | You tell a great joke. | C | T |
| 5. | Your bike gets a flat tire. | C | T |
| 6. | You play a harmless trick on your teacher. | C | T |

Tell about **two comic events** and **two tragic events** in your life. *A total of 4 points is possible on this section.*

Comic events in my life:

1.


2.


Tragic events in my life:

1.


2.

Your score = _____
Possible points ___10___

# MASK RATING SCALE

1. Decoration (A total of 6 points is possible)

    Presence of multiple features      (2 Points)      _____

    Variety of materials used      (2 Points)      _____

    Visual appeal      (2 Points)      _____

2. Creativity (A total of 6 points is possible)

    Characterization      (2 Points)      _____

    Color choice      (2 Points)      _____

    Novelty      (2 Points)      _____

3. Neatness (A total of 6 points is possible)

    Proper use of glue and scissors      (2 Points)      _____

    Application of decorative materials      (2 Points)      _____

    Paint quality      (2 Points)      _____

Your Score = _____
Possible points     18

# Egg Rating Scale

**Project:** _____

**Components:**

1. Designs (color, form, texture, and so on)    2 points possible    —————

2. Neatness (cutting, painting, gluing, and so on)  2 points possible    —————

3. Creativity    2 points possible    —————

4. Visual Appeal    2 points possible    —————

5. Color Choice (variety, vividness, and so on)  2 points possible    —————

Student Score = _____

Total Possible Points =   10

**Name:** _____ **Date:** _____

## Here's what I thought!!!

1. This project was:


2. I liked it because:


3. I didn't like it because:


4. I'm proud of my work because:


5. If we did this again, I would:


6. I learned that:


7. Additional comments:

# Assessments for Chapter Five: How's the Weather?

## Rubric For Expert Written Report of Weather

Expert written reports will be graded on a scale from 5 to 0 on the basis of the following criteria:

**5**    All four of the following topics are included in the report:
Where this particular weather condition occurs
Why this weather occurs (how it forms)
What damage this weather can do
A general description of what this weather condition is
In addition, few grammatical errors exist, and sentence structure is well-organized.

**4**    Three of the four above topics are included, few grammatical errors exist, and sentence order is well-organized.

**3**    Three of the four above topics are included, but grammatical errors and/or disorganized sentence structure reduces comprehension.
(or) Two of the four above topics are included, and few grammatical errors exist, and sentence order is well organized.

**2**    Two of the four above topics are included, and grammatical errors and/or disorganized sentence structure reduces comprehension.

**1**    One of the four above topics is included, and grammatical errors and/or disorganized sentence structure reduces comprehension.

**0**    None of the above topics is included.

*Student Name:* _____

*Weather condition reported upon:* _____

*Date of report:* _____

*Score:* _____

# Rating Scale for Oral Report of Weather

Each item is worth a maximum of three points.  Total points possible = 27

## Voice

_____  Student's voice projected at a level audible across the room.

_____  Student spoke slowly and comprehensibly.

_____  Student's voice had appropriate inflection.

## Body Language

_____  Student made eye contact with audience.

_____  Student had overall composure during presentation.

_____  Student remained in front of audience until entire presentation was completed.

## Information

_____  Student delivered report with little or no reference to notes.

_____  Student remembered all four topics to be presented.

_____  Student report was within the time frame of 2-4 minutes.

## Extra bonus points may be awarded for an area in which the student excelled.

_____  Points are awarded for: _____

_Student Name:_ _____

_Weather condition reported upon:_ _____

_Date of report:_ _____

_Total Score:_ _____

# Rating Scale For Cultural Presentation

Each item is worth up to three points. Total points possible = 27

## Voice

_____ Student's voice projected at a level audible across the room.

_____ Student spoke slowly and comprehensibly.

_____ Student's voice had appropriate inflection.

## Information

_____ Student delivered relevant information that showed sensitivity toward the culture being presented.

_____ Information was detailed.

_____ Information presented tied culture to weather.

## Visual

_____ Student's choice of visual enhanced understanding of the presentation.

_____ Student put quality time into visual.

_____ Visual was authentic. It had characteristics true to the cultural component being discussed.

**Extra bonus points** may be awarded for an area in which the student excelled.

_____ Points are awarded for: _____

*Student Name:* _____

*Culture reported upon:* _____

*Date of report:* _____

*Total Score:* _____

## Rating Scale For Outline Of Role-Playing Activity

Each item is worth a maximum of 4 points. Total points possible: 20

In your outline, how well do you...

_____introduce who you are.  Give a little background on yourself.

_____express your position on global warming.  Explain how deforestation is affecting you.

_____present your position with facts and personal feelings.

_____include detailed arguments in your favor.

_____get others in your group to understand your position. They may not change their minds, but did they see your point of view?

*Student Name:* _____   *Role adopted:* _____

*Date of outline:* _____   *Total Score:* _____

## Checklist for Journal Responses

Student Name:

| Lesson number | Prompt | Did respond | Did not respond |
|---|---|---|---|
| Three | Huichol Indians | | |
| Six | Tornado fears | | |
| Seven | Origin legend | | |
| Eight | Hurricane, monsoon or typhoon? | | |
| Nine | Water list | | |
| Thirteen | Lowering $CO_2$ emissions | | |

## End of the Unit Exam

Student name: _____ Date: _____

*Questions 1-8 are worth 5 points each.*

1.    In your own words, define culture.


2.    List five aspects of culture we have studied in this unit.


3.    Compare the terms "climate" and "weather."


4.    What are some ways weather and climate affect culture?


5.    Describe one way climate affected the culture of the Inuit People.


6.    Describe one way climate affected the culture of the Huichol people.


7.    Choose one type of storm, or drought, that we studied in class.  Explain where
      this type of weather occurs, how it forms, and what type of damage it can do.



8.    List a global issue, problem, or aspect of culture that we studied from more
      than one perspective.  Briefly explain the points of view studied.



*Please choose to answer question A or question B.  This question will be worth 10
   points.  Use the back of this paper to write your answer.*

A.  Discuss the ozone depletion problem.   Include the following information in
     your answer.  What are some of its causes?  Who is it affecting?  Where is it
     occurring?  How can we prevent it from continuing?

B.  Define global warming.   Include the following information in your answer.
     Where is it occurring?  What are some of its causes?  Who is it affecting?
     How can we prevent it from continuing ?

# Student Evaluation of Multicultural Meteorology Unit

Describe some of the lessons that you particularly enjoyed.

Discuss some concepts, facts, etc., that you learned from this unit.

Discuss any lessons that you did not enjoy. Tell what you disliked, and how I could improve it for next year's class.

Overall, do you think the unit was at the right academic level for you? That is, was it difficult enough that you learned something, too difficult, or too easy? Explain.

What did the unit teach you about culture and people that you did not know before? Explain.

Did the unit change your opinion about any group of people, global issue, or environmental problem in the world today? Explain.

Discuss anything else about the unit you feel I should know.

# Assessments for Chapter Six:  We the People...

Date: _____

Discussion Topic:

_____

## CLASSROOM DISCUSSION SCORE SHEET

| Observable Indicators | Often | Sometimes | Never |
|---|---|---|---|
| 1. Students are on task. | | | |
| 2. Students ask questions and make comments related to the topics. | | | |
| 3. Students accept diverse points of view and opinions. | | | |
| 4. Students can draw meaningful conclusions from their discussion. | | | |
| 5. Students' discussion indicates understanding of the material. | | | |
| 6. Students listen attentively to others. | | | |

**Comments:**

Name: _____
Date: _____
Assignment: _____

# STUDENT WRITING RUBRIC:
# PROBLEM-SOLVING ASSIGNMENTS

4   Presents a sound understanding of the concept and the assignment. States the problems clearly. Provides logical, well-developed, and well-thought out resolutions to the   problems. The resolutions reflect creative thinking as well as thoughtful attention to the details of the problems.

3   Presents a clear statement of the problems and resolutions to the problems associated with the assignment. The resolutions are a logical and plausible outcome of the problems.

2   States the problems effectively. Develops and presents at least one resolution to the problems associated with the assignment. The resolution is satisfactory, but lacks thorough treatment and accuracy.

1   Presents no resolutions or presents unsubstantiated and implausible resolutions to the problems, and indicates little understanding of the assignment and the problems at hand.

Comments:

Name: _____
Date: _____
Activity: _____

## RUBRIC FOR
## WORKING TOWARD THE ACHIEVEMENT OF GROUP GOALS

4  Actively helps identify group goals and works hard to meet them.

3  Communicates commitment to the group goals and effectively carries out assigned roles.

2  Communicates a commitment to the group goals but does not carry out assigned roles.

1  Does not work toward group goals or actually works against them.

**Comments:**

Name: _____
Date: _____
Activity: _____

## RUBRIC FOR CHOOSING ALTERNATIVES TO MEET THE ESTABLISHED CRITERIA

**4**  Selects alternatives that meet or exceed the criteria and that represent a well-supported answer to the initial discussion question.

**3**  Successfully answers the discussion question by selecting alternatives that meet or exceed established criteria.

**2**  Selects alternatives that do not entirely conform to the established criteria.

**1**  Makes a selection that does not appear reasonable or cannot be justified by the student's evaluation of the established criteria.

**Comments:**

Group: _____
Date: _____
Activity: _____

# COOPERATIVE GROUPWORK OBSERVATION CHECKLIST

*OBSERVABLE INDICATOR*          *OFTEN   SOMETIMES   NEVER*

1.  Students are on task.

2.  Students listen attentively
    to others.

3.  Students respond to each
    other.

4.  Students help others
    analyze and solve problems.

5.  Students are accepting and
    encouraging of others in the
    group.

6.  Students can justify and
    explain their responses.

7.  The group shares equally in
    the task at hand.

**Comments:**

Name: _____

Date: _____

# CHECKLIST FOR STUDENT PERFORMANCE: "YANKEE DOODLE" BIOGRAPHICAL SONG

_____ You used the proper tune.

_____ You sang loudly, slowly, and clearly.

_____ You showed enthusiasm.

_____ You included pertinent biographical information.

_____ Optional: You created more than one verse.

*GRADING SCALE:*          *YOUR GRADE:* _____

4 or 5 out of 4:  +
2 or 3 out of 4:  ✓
0 or 1 out of 4:  −

**Comments:**

Copyright © 1998 by Allyn and Bacon

W W W W W W

Name: _____
Date: _____

# RUBRIC FOR
# ASSESSING KNOWLEDGE OF THE "FIVE W'S"

+ Able to pick out the essential points of the article as assigned. Four or five of the items are correct.

✓ Able to pick out several of the essential points as assigned. Two or three of the items are correct.

– Had difficulty picking out the essential points of the article as assigned. One or none of the items is correct.

**Comments:**

**Your Score:** _____

Name: _____

Date: _____

Assignment: _____

# STUDENT WRITING RUBRIC: PROVIDING INFORMATION ON A GIVEN TOPIC

4  Provides accurate information on the topic at hand.  The facts, concepts or principles used are appropriate to the topic and effectively explained.  The information reflects thorough and careful research and understanding.

3  Provides accurate information on the topic at hand.  The facts, concepts or principles used are appropriate to the topic and adequately applied, with no significant errors.

2  Explains the topic at hand but misapplies or omits some facts, concepts or principles that are important for the understanding of the topic.

1  Leaves out key facts, concepts, or principles in explaining the topic, or does not use appropriate facts, concepts or principles to explain the topic.

Comments:

## Assessments for Chapter Seven: Maya and Aztec

Name: _____

# Maya and Aztec Project Evaluation Sheet

Each project is rated on a scale from 1 to 4 on the basis of the following criteria:

4 = Product displays top quality work which is complete and demonstrates thorough understanding of the aspect highlighted.

3 = Product displays above average work which is complete and/or demonstrates good understanding of the aspect highlighted.

2 = Product displays average quality work which is slightly incomplete and/or demonstrates an incomplete understanding of the aspect highlighted.

1 = Product displays poor quality work which is incomplete and/or demonstrates a lack of understanding of the aspect highlighted.

1. **Timeline**                                    4   3   2   1

2. **Pyramid silhouette**                          4   3   2   1

3. **Mural scene and facts**                       4   3   2   1

4. **Independent writing activity**                4   3   2   1
   (Personal legend)

5. **Warrior headdress**                           4   3   2   1

6. **Mosaic mask**                                 4   3   2   1

7. **Mayan Dance of the Reeds**                    4   3   2   1

8. **Patolli game**                                4   3   2   1
   (Group is evaluated together)

9. **Hieroglyph writing activity**                 4   3   2   1

10. **Passport entries**                           4   3   2   1

_____    **Total Points**

Name: _____

# Maya and Aztec Essay Quiz

**1. The Maya and the Aztec were true civilizations. Explain their five basic characteristics which distinguished them as civilizations: their stable food supply, specialization of labor, system of government, social levels, and a highly developed culture that included art, architecture, religion, music and law.**

Responses will be rated on a scale from 1 to 4 on the basis of the following criteria:

4 = Response develops all five characteristics in an organized and thorough way.

3 = Response mentions at least four of the five characteristics and/or may be somewhat disorganized or slightly incomplete.

2 = Response mentions only three of the five characteristics and/or may be disorganized or incomplete.

1 = Response mentions only one or two of the five characteristics in a disorganized and incomplete manner.

**2. Discuss your favorite part or parts of this unit. Give details of the projects you completed, why you liked them, and what you learned from them.**

Responses will be rated on a scale from 1 to 4 on the basis of the following criteria:

4 = Response is descriptive, complete, and thoroughly explains the rationale for why the project was liked and what was learned from it.

3 = Response is occasionally descriptive, somewhat complete, and/or basically explains the rationale for why the project was liked and what was learned from it.

2 = Response lacks description, is incomplete, and/or only superficially explains the rationale for why the project was liked and what was learned from it.

1 = Response is not descriptive, is incomplete, and/or does not explain the rationale for why the project was liked and what was learned from it.

# REFERENCE APPENDIX

## Chapter One: When the shoe won't fit...

Arreaga-Mayer, C., & Greenwood, C. R. (1986). Environmental variables affecting school achievement. National Association of Bilingual Education Journal, 10 (2), 113-136.

Bagin, D., Gallagher, D. R., & Kindred, L. W. (1994). The school and community relations (5th ed.). Boston, MA: Allyn and Bacon.

Bamberger, R. (1974). Literacy and development in reading. In J. Merritt (Ed.), New horizons in reading. Newark, DE: International Reading Association.

Banks, J. A. (1991). Teaching strategies for ethnic studies (5th ed.). Boston, MA: Allyn and Bacon.

Banks, J. A. (1994). Multiethnic education: Theory and practice (3rd ed.). Boston, MA: Allyn and Bacon.

Banks, J. A. (1995). Multicultural education: Historical development, dimensions, and practice. In J. A. Banks and C. A. McGee Banks (Eds.), Handbook of research on multicultural education (pp. 3-24). New York, NY: MacMillan.

Bissex, G. (1988). The beginnings of writing. In B. Fillion, C. Hedley, & E. Dimartino (Eds.), Home and school: Early language and reading (pp. 47-63). Norwood, N. J.: Ablex.

Brown, A. L., & Campione, J. C. (1981). Inducing flexible thinking: A problem of access. In M. Friedman, J. P. Dast & N. O'Conner (Eds.), Intelligence and learning (pp. 515-524). New York, NY: Plenum Press.

Cazden, C. (1983). Peekaboo as an instructional model: Discourse development at home and at school. In B. Bain (Ed.), The sociogenesis of language and human conduct (pp. 38-58). New York, NY: Plenum.

Cazden, C. (1985). The social context of learning to read. In H. Singer and R. B. Ruddell (Eds.), Theoretical models and processes of reading (3rd ed.), (pp. 595-610). Newark, DE: International Reading Association.

Cochran-Smith, M. (1986). Reading to children: A model for understanding text. In B. Schieffelin & P. Gilmore (Eds.), The acquisition of literacy: Ethnographic perspectives (pp. 35-54). Norwood, N. J.: Ablex.

Cortes, C. (March, 1995). Backing into the future: Teaching and learning in and for a changing multicultural world. Distinguished lecture on critical issues presented at the national conference of the Association for Supervision and Curriculum Development, San Fransisco, CA.

Cummins, J. (1986). Empowering minority students: A framework for intervention. Harvard Educational Review, 56, 18-36.

Elkind, D. (1995). School and family in the Postmodern world. Phi Delta Kappan, 77 (1), 8-14.

Epstein, J. (1995). School/family/community partnerships: Caring for the children we share. Phi Delta Kappan, 76 (9), 701-712.

Fillion, B. (1988). School influences on the language of children. In B. Fillion, C. Hedley, & E. Dimartino (Eds.), Home and school: Early language and reading (pp. 155-168). Norwood, N. J.: Ablex.

Fisher, F. (1965). The influence of reading and discussion on the attitudes of fifth graders toward American Indians. Unpublished doctoral dissertation, University of California, Berkeley.

Gay, G. (1995). Curriculum theory and multicultural education. In J. A. Banks and C. A. McGee Banks (Eds.), Handbook of research on multicultural education (pp. 25-43). New York, NY: MacMillan.

Goodman, J. (1995). Change without difference: School restructuring in historical perspective. Harvard Educational Review, 65 (1),1-29.

Grant, C. A., & Sleeter, C. E. (1989). Turning on learning: Five approaches for multicultural teaching plans for race, class, gender, and disability. New York, NY: MacMillan.

Hayes, M. L., & Conklin, M. E. (1953). Intergroup attitudes and experimental change. Journal of Experimental Education, 22, 19-36.

Heath, S. B. (1983). Ways with words: Language, life and work in communities and classrooms. Cambridge, ENG: Cambridge University Press.

Heath, S. B. (1986). Separating "things of the imagination" from life: Learning to read and write. In W. Teale & E. Sulzby (Eds.), Emergent literacy (pp. 156-172). Norwood, N. J.: Ablex.

Lee, H. (1960). To kill a mockingbird. Philadelphia, PA: Lippincott.

Leslie, L. L., & Leslie, J. W. (1972). The effects of a student centered special curriculum upon the racial attitudes of sixth graders. Journal of Experimental Education, 41, 63-67.

Lessing, E. E., & Clarke, C. (1976). An attempt to reduce ethnic prejudice and assess its correlates. Educational Research Quarterly, 1, 3-16.

Lichter, J. H., & Johnson, D. W. (1969). Changes in attitudes toward Negroes of White elementary school students after use of multiethnic readers. Journal of Educational Psychology, 60, 148-152.

Lichter, J. H., Johnson, D. W., & Ryan, F. L. (1973). Use of pictures of multiethnic interaction to change attitudes of White elementary school students toward Blacks. Psychological Reports, 33, 367-372.

Munsch, R. (1980). The paper bag princess. Canada: Annick Press, Ltd.

Noddings, N. (1995). A morally defensible mission for schools in the 21st century. Phi Delta Kappan, 76 (5), 365-368.

Norton, D. E. (1991). Through the eyes of a child: An introduction to children's literature (3rd ed.). New York, NY: MacMillan.

Odden, E. R. & Wohlstetter, P. (1995). Making school-based management work. Educational Leadership, 52 (5), 32-36.

Scieszka, J. (1989). The true story of the three little pigs. New York, NY: Penguin Books.

Shirley, O. L. B. (1988). The impact of multicultural education on self-concept, racial attitude and student achievement of Black and White fifth and sixth graders. Unpublished doctoral dissertation, University of Mississippi.

Sleeter, C. E., & Grant, C. A.  (1994).  <u>Making choices for multicultural education:</u> <u>Five approaches to race, class, and gender</u> (2nd ed.).  New York, NY: MacMillan.

Taylor, D. (1988).  The (con) textual worlds of childhood:  An interpretive approach to alternative dimensions of experience.  In B. Fillion, C. Hedley, & E. Dimartino (Eds.), <u>Home and school: Early language and reading</u> (pp. 93-107). Norwood, N. J.: Ablex.

Tharp, R. G., & Gallimore, R. (1988).  <u>Rousing minds to life: Teaching, learning and</u> <u>schooling in social context.</u>  Cambridge, ENG: Cambridge University Press.

Trager, H. G., & Yarrow, M. R. (1952).  <u>They learn what they live: Prejudice in young</u> <u>children</u>.  New York, NY: Harper & Brothers.

Wells, G. (1985).  Preschool literacy-related activities and success in school.  In D. Olson, N. Torrance, & A. Hildyard (Eds.), <u>Literacy, language, and learning:</u> <u>The nature and consequences of reading and writing</u> (pp. 229-255). Cambridge, ENG: Cambridge University Press.

World of Difference anti-bias curriculum.  Available from the Anti-Defamation League, 823 United Nations Plaza, New York, NY 10017.

Yawkey, T. D. (1973).  Attitudes toward Black Americans held by rural and urban White early childhood subjects based upon multi-ethnic social studies materials. <u>Journal of Negro Education, 42,</u> 164-169.

# Chapter Two:  Quilts, knots, and journeys

## Professional resources

Banks, James. (1991) . <u>Teaching strategies for ethnic studies</u> ( 5th ed. ). Boston, MA: Allyn and Bacon.

Berger, Eugenia.  (1995).  <u>Parents as partners in education:  Families and schools</u> <u>working together</u> ( 4th ed. ). Columbus, OH: Prentice Hall.

Bunting, Eve.  (1988).  <u>How many days to America? A Thanksgiving story</u>.  New York, NY: Clarion Books.

Burk, D., Snider, A., & Symonds, P. (1991).  <u>Math excursions 2:  Project-based</u> <u>mathematics for second graders</u>. Portsmouth, NH: Heinemann.

Coerr, Eleanor. (1986).  <u>The Josefina story quilt</u>. New York, NY: Harper Collins.

Flournoy, Valerie. (1985).  <u>The patchwork quilt</u>. New York, NY: E. P. Dutton.

Gonsalves, Alyson S. (Eds.). ( 1974 ). <u>Quilting & patchwork</u>. Menlo Park, CA:  Lane Books.

Grant, C. A.  & Sleeter, C.E. (1989).  <u>Turning on learning:  Five approaches for</u> <u>multicultural teaching plans for race, class, gender and disability</u>. New York, NY: Merrill.

Imdieke, Sandra. J. (1990).  Sharing Stories:  Multicultural traditions.  Paper presented at the annual meeting of the International Reading Association, Atlanta, GA.

Levinson, Riki. (1985). <u>Watch the stars come out</u>. New York, NY: E. P. Dutton.

Martin, B., Jr., & Archambault, J. (1987).  <u>Knots on a Counting Rope</u>.  New York, NY: Henry Holt and Company.

McCabe, Allyssa. (1992). All kinds of good stories. Paper presented at the annual meeting of the National Reading Conference, San Antonio, TX.

Norton, Donna E. (1991). Through the eyes of a child: An introduction to children's literature. New York, NY: MacMillan.

Pellowski, Anne. (1987). The family storytelling handbook. New York, NY: MacMillan.

Say, Allen. (1993). Grandfather's Journey. New York, NY: Scholastic Inc.

Sleeter, C. E. & Grant, C. E. (1993). Making choices for multicultural education: Five approaches to race, class, and gender (2nd ed.). New York, NY: Merrill.

Suratm Michele M. (1983). Angel child, dragon child. New York, NY: Scholastic Inc.

Takaki, Ronald. (1993). A different mirror: A history of multicultural America. Boston, MA: Little, Brown and Company.

Wecksler, Margo A. (1989). Moving toward a multi-ethnic perspective. (ERIC Document Reproduction Service No. ED 309 406).

Wolff, Leanne O. (1993). Family narrative: How stories shape us. Paper presented at the annual meeting of the Speech Communication Association, Miami Beach, FL.

## Stories About Quilts

Coerr, Eleanor. (1986). The Josefina story quilt. New York, NY: Harper Collins.

Ernst, Lisa C. (1983). Sam Johnson and the blue ribbon quilt. New York, NY: Lothrop, Lee, and Shepard.

Flournoy, Valerie. (1985). The patchwork quilt. New York, NY: E. P. Dutton.

Johnston, Tony. (1985). The quilt story. New York, NY: Scholastic, Inc.

Polacco, Patricia. (1988). The keeping quilt. New York, NY: Simon and Schuster Books For Young Readers.

## Children and Grandparents

Bunting, Eve. (1989). The Wednesday surprise. Clarion Books, New York.

Gilman, Phoebe. (1992). Something from nothing. New York, NY: Scholastic, Inc.

Martin, B., Jr., and Archambault, J. (1987). Knots on a counting rope. New York, NY: Henry Holt and Company.

Medearis, Angela S. (1991). Dancing with the Indians. New York, NY: Scholastic, Inc.

Polacco, Patricia. (1992). Mrs. Katz and Tush. New York, NY: Bantam Books for Young Readers.

Rylant, Cynthia. (1982). When I was young in the mountains. New York, NY: E.P. Dutton.

Say, Allen. (1993). Grandfather's journey. New York, NY: Scholastic Inc.

Tompert, Ann. (1990). Grandfather Tang's story: A tale told with tangrams. New York, NY: Crown Publishers, Inc.

## Naming Stories

Martin, B., Jr, and Archambault, J. (1987). <u>Knots on a counting rope</u>. New York, NY: Henry Holt and Company.

Mosel, Arlene. (1968). <u>Tikki Tikki Tembo</u>. New York, NY: Holt, Rinehart & Winston.

Suratm, Michele M. (1983). <u>Angel child, dragon child</u>. New York, NY: Scholastic Inc.

## Stories About Coming to America

Bunting, Eve. (1988). <u>How many days to America? A Thanksgiving story</u>. New York, NY: Clarion Books.

Levinson, Riki. (1985). <u>Watch the stars come out</u>. New York, NY: E. P. Dutton.

Say, Allen. (1993). <u>Grandfather's journey</u>. New York, NY: Scholastic Inc.

Suratm Michele M. (1983). <u>Angel child, dragon child</u>. New York, NY: Scholastic Inc.

## Families Pass on Traditions

Friedman, Ina. (1984). <u>How my parents learned to eat</u>. Boston, MA: Houghton Mifflin Company.

Polacco, Patricia. (1992). <u>Mrs. Katz and Tush</u>. New York: Dell Publishing.

Waters, K. and Slovnez-Low, M. (1990). <u>Lion dancer: Ernie Wan's Chinese New Year</u>. New York, NY: Scholastic, Inc.

# Chapter Three: Celebrations with a twist

Banks, J. A. (1988). Approaches to Multicultural Curriculum Reform. <u>Multicultural Leader, 1</u> (2).

Banks, J. A. (1991). <u>Teaching strategies for ethnic studies</u> (5th ed.). Boston: Allyn and Bacon.

Barcher, S. I. (1993). <u>Readers' theatre for beginning readers</u>. Englewood, NJ: Teacher Ideas Press.

Barr, M. G. (1995). <u>International spring and summer festivals</u>. Carthage, NY: Good Apple.

Cohen, B. (1983). <u>Molly's pilgrim</u>. New York, NY: Lothrop, Lee & Shepard Books.

Coskey, E. (1973). <u>Easter eggs for everyone</u>. Nashville, TN: Abingdon Press.

D'Amato, J., & D'Amato, A. (1969). <u>African crafts for you to make</u>. New York, NY: Julian Messner.

Glubok, S. (1975). <u>Dolls, dolls, dolls</u>. Chicago, IL: Follett Publishing Co.

Gollnick, D. M. & Chinn, P. C. (1994). <u>Multicultural education in a pluralistic society</u> (4th ed.). New York, NY: Macmillan College Publishing Co.

Hunt, K., & Carlson, B. W. (1961). <u>Masks and mask makers</u>. Nashville, TN: Abingdon Press.

Menendez, A. (1994). Christmas in the schools: Can conflict be avoided? <u>Educational Leadership</u>, 239-242.

Sandu, D. S., & Rigney, J. R. (1995). Culturally responsive teaching in the U.S. public schools. Kappan, 161.

Sleeter, C. E. & Grant, C. E. (1993). Making choices for multicultural education: Five approaches to race, class, and gender (2nd ed.). New York, NY: Merrill.

Terzian, A. M. (1993). The kids' multicultural art book. Charlotte, VT: Williamson Publishing Company.

Tiedt, P. L., & Teidt, I. M. (1990). Multicultural teaching (3rd ed.). Boston, MA: Allyn and Bacon.

Thomas, M. (1974). Free to be... you and me. New York, NY: Bantam Books.

Zolotow, C. (1972). Williams' doll. New York, NY: Harper & Row.

# Chapter Four: Domo Arigato

Ackley, M., & Weber, V. (1989). Children of the world: Japan. Milwaukee, WI: Gareth Stevens Publishing.

Allen, Carol. (1992). Japan: Traditions and trends. New York, NY: Simon & Schuster.

Araki, C. (1965). Origami in the classroom: Activities for autumn through Christmas (Vol. I). Rutland, VT: C. E. Tuttle.

Araki, C. (1968). Origami in the classroom: Activities for winter through summer (Vol. II). Rutland, VT: C. E. Tuttle.

Carnes, J. (1995). Home was a horse stall. Teaching Tolerance, 4 (1), 57.

Haskins, Jim. (1987). Count your way through Japan. Minneapolis, MN: Carolrhoda Books, Inc.

Jacobsen, Karen. (1982). A new true book: Japan. Chicago, IL: Children's Press.

Japan: World neighbor series (1994). Cypress, NY: Creative Teaching Press,

Kallevig, P. (1991). Folding stories: Storytelling and origami together as one. Newburgh, IN: Storytime Ink International.

Kalman, Bobbie. (1989). Japan: The people. Toronto, NY: Crabtree Publishing Company.

Maher, J., & Selwyn, D. (1993). Japanese Americans. Seattle, WA: Turman Publishing Co.

Mosel, Arlene. (1972). The funny little woman. New York, NY: E.P. Dutton.

Sakurai, Gail. (1994). Peach Boy. Mahwah, NJ: Troll Associates.

Say, Allen. (1993). Grandfather's Journey. New York, NY: Scholastic Inc.

SchoolDays, (1986 & 1995). April, May, June issues of 1986; April, May, June issues of 1995, Torrance, CA: Frank Schaffer Publications.

Suyenaga, Ruth. (1993). Obon. Cleveland, OH: Modern Curriculum Press.

Tames, Richard. (1991). Journey Through Japan. Mahwah, NJ: Troll Associates.

# Chapter Five: How's the weather?

Aardema, V. (1981). Bringing the rain to Kapiti plain. New York, NY: Dial Books for Young Readers.

Atwater, M., Baptiste, P., Daniel, L., Hackett, J., Moyer, R., Takemoto, C., & Wilson, N. (1993). Oceans of air (Teacher's ed.). New York, NY: MacMillan/McGraw-Hill School Publishing Company.

Barrett, J. (1978). Cloudy with a chance of meatballs. New York, NY: Aladdin Paperbacks.

Bernhard, E. (1994). The tree that rains: The flood myth of the Huichol indians of Mexico. NewYork, NY: Holiday House.

Bryan, A. (1993). The story of lightning and thunder. New York: Athenium.

Flagler, T.B., Heigl, R., May, T.T., Paxton, E., Weisbach, W.S.V., & Shemie, B. (1989). Houses of snow, skin and bones. Montreal, Canada: Tundra Books.

Harshman, M. (1995). The storm. NewYork, NY: Cobblehill Books

Harrell, B. O. (1995). How thunder and lightning came to be. New York, NY: Dial Books for Young Readers.

May, T. T., & Paxton, E. (1990). Windows on science: earth science (Vol. 1, 2, and 3). [videodisc-based curriculum program]. Warren, NJ:

Simon, S. (1989). Storms. New York, NY: Scholastic Inc.

Smith, H. E. (1990). Weather. New York, NY: MacMillan/McGraw-Hill School Publishing Company.

Wiesner, D. (1990). Hurricane. New York, NY: Clarion Books.

Wisniewski, D. (1991). Rain Player. New York, NY: Clarion Books.

Wurzel, J. (1988). Toward multiculturalism: a reader in multicultural education. Yarmouth, ME: Intercultural Press, Inc.

Zolotow, C. (1995). When the wind stops. New York, NY: Harper Collins Publishers.

# Chapter Six: We the people...

Adler, S. (1983, November). What is social studies? Student teacher perspectives. Paper presented at the National Council for the Social Studies, San Francisco, CA.

America will be. (1991). Boston, MA: Houghton Mifflin Co.

Aten, J. (1987). Our living constitution. Carthage, IL: Good Apple, Inc.

Aten, J. (1989). Democracy for young Americans. Carthage, IL: Good Apple, Inc.

Banks, J. A. (1991). Teaching strategies for ethnic studies. Boston, MA: Allyn and Bacon.

Carroll, P.N. & Noble, D.W. (1977). The free and the unfree. New York, NY: Penguin Books.

Crabtree, C. & Nash, G.B. (Eds.) (1994). National standards for United States history: Exploring the American experience, grades 5-12. National Center for History in the Schools.

Davis, K. C. (1990). Don't know much about history. New York, NY: Avon Books.

The Education Center, Inc. (November/December, 1993). The intermediate mailbox.

The Education Center, Inc. (February/March, 1994). The teacher's helper.

Fischer, M. W. (1993). American history simulations. Huntington Beach, CA: Teacher Created Materials, Inc.

Grant, C. A. & Sleeter, C. E. (1989). Turning on learning. New York, NY: Macmillan Publishing.

Marzano, J., Pickering, D., & McTighe, J. (1993). Assessing student outcomes. Alexandria, VA: Association for Supervision and Curriculum Development.

Merton, R.K. (1972). Insiders and outsiders: A chapter in the sociology of knowledge. The American Journal of Sociology, 78 (1), 9-47.

Patrick. J.J. & Leming, R.S. (1991). Resources for teachers on the Bill of Rights. Commission on the Bicentennial of the United States Constitution.

Shenkman, R. (1991). I love Paul Revere, whether he rode or not. New York, NY: Harper Collins.

Shenkman, R. (1988). Legends, lies and cherished myths of American history. New York, NY: William Morrow and Co.

Smith, G. (1978). Teaching about United States history: a comparative approach. Center for Teaching International Relations at the University of Denver.

Takaki, R. (1993). A different mirror: A history of multicultural America. Boston, MA: Little, Brown and Co.

Thornton, S.J. (1990, April). Perspectives on teaching and learning history, or "They could have thrown teapots for all I care." Paper presented at the annual meeting of the American Educational Research Association, Boston, MA.

Voices in African American history: The American revolution. (1994). Cleveland, OH: Modern Curriculum Press.

We the people... (1989). Calabasas, CA: Center for Civic Education.

Zinn, H. (1980). A people's history of the United States. New York, NY: Harper Collins.

## Chapter Seven: Maya and Aztec

Baquedano, E. (1993). Aztec, Inca and Maya. New York, NY: Alfred A. Knopf.

Berdan, F. F. (1982). The Aztecs of central Mexico. New York, NY: Holt, Rinehart & Winston.

Bray, W. (1987). Everyday life of the Aztecs. New York, NY: Dorset.

The Mayan: Apocalypse Then. (Video). Distributed by Barr Films.

Flora, S. B. (1993). Multicultural Mini-Units. Grand Rapids, Michigan: T.S. Dennison and Co.

Gallenkamp, S. (1976). Maya: The riddle and rediscovery of a lost civilization. New York, NY: Penguin Books.

Morley, S. G. (1956). The Ancient Maya. (Revised by George W. Brainerd). Stanford, CA: Stanford University Press.

Parke, M., & Panik, S. (1994). A Quetzalcoatl Tale of Chocolate (book and teacher's guide). Carthage, IL: Fearon Teacher Aids.

Stohl, M., & Schneck, S. (1994). Maya Aztecs Incas. New York, NY: Scholastic.

Vaillant, G. C. (1965). Aztecs of Mexico: Origin, rise, and fall of the Aztec nation. New York, NY: Penguin Books.

Whitlock, R. (1976). Everyday life of the Maya. New York, NY: Dorset Press.

## Chapter Eight: A multicultural literary guide

Audiovisual Resource Guide: 1994-96 Elementary Level (1994). San Diego, CA: San Diego County Office of Education.

Banks, J. A. (1991). Teaching strategies for ethnic studies (5th ed.), (pp. 155-156). Boston, MA: Allyn & Bacon.

Barber, B. R. (1992). An aristocracy of everyone. New York, NY: Oxford University Press.

Carnes, J. (1995). Home was a horse stall. Teaching Tolerance, 4 (1), 57.

Dewey, J. (1966). Democracy and education. Toronto, Ontario: MacMillan.

Grant, C. A. & Sleeter, C. E. (1989). Turning on learning: Five approaches for multicultural teaching plans for race, class, gender, and disability. New York, NY: Merrill.

Grant, C. A. & Sleeter, C. E. (1993). Making choices for multicultural education: Five approaches to race, class, and gender (2nd ed.). New York, NY: Merrill.

Helbig, A. K. & Perkins, A. G. (1994). This land is our land: A guide to multicultural literature for children. Westport, CT: Greenwood Press.

Lazear, D. (1994). Multiple intelligence approaches to assessment: Solving the assessment conundrum. Tucson, AZ: Zephyr.

Miller-Lachmann (1992). Our family, our friends, our world: An annotated guide to significant multicultural books for children and teenagers. New Providence, NY: R. R. Bowker.

Nieto, S. (1992). Affirming diversity: The sociopolitical context of multicultural education. New York, NY: Longman.

Rasinski, T. V. & Gillespie, C. S. (1992). Sensitive issues: An annotated guide to children's literature K-6. Phoenix, AZ: Oryx.

Schon, I. (1991). A Hispanic heritage: A guide to juvenile books about Hispanic people and cultures. Metuchen, NJ & London, ENG: Scarecrow Press.

Stapin, B. & Seale, D. (Eds). (1989). Books without bias: Through Indian eyes. Beverly, CA: Oyate.

Yokota, J. (1993). Issues in selecting multicultural children's literature. Language Arts, 70, 156-167.

## Professional Resources for Selecting Children's Literature

Barstow, B., and Riggle, J. (1995). Beyond picture books (2nd. ed.). New Providence, NY: Bowker

Bookbird: World of children's books. The journal of IBBY, the International Board on Books for Young People. Available through the Department of Foreign Languages and Literature, 138 Stanley Coulter Hall, Purdue University, West Lafayette, Indiana 47907-1359.

Dreyer, B. (1981). The book finder: A guide to children's literature about the needs and problems of youth aged 2 to 15 (Vols. I & II). Circle Pines, MN: American Guidance Service, Inc.

Freeman, J. (1995). More books kids will sit still for. New Providence, NY: Bowker.

Hayden, C. D. (Ed.). Venturing into cultures: A resource book of multicultural materials and programs. Chicago, IL: American Library Association.

Huck, C. (1979). Children's literature in the elementary school (3rd. ed.). New York, NY: Holt, Rinehart & Winston.

Jeff-Simpson, M. (Ed.). (1989). Adventuring with books: A booklist for pre-K to Grade 6. Urbana, IL: National Council of Teachers of English.

Multicultural Review. Greenwood Publishing Group, 88 Post Road West, P. O. Box

5007, Westport, CT 06881-5007

Reed, A. (1988). <u>Comics to classics: A parent's guide to books for teens and preteens</u>. Newark, DE: International Reading Association.

Spirit, D. L. (1988). <u>Introducing bookplots 3: A book talk guide for use with readers ages 8 to 12.</u> New York, NY: R. R. Bowker.

Trelease, J. (1985). <u>The read-aloud handbook</u>. New York, NY: Penguin.

Tway, E. (Ed.). (1981). <u>Reading ladders for human relations</u> (6th ed.). Washington, D. C.: American Coucnil on Education.

## Children's literature reviewed in the guide

Adler, D. (1989). <u>Jackie Robinson: He was the first.</u> New York, NY: Holiday. ISBN 0-8234-0743-9.

Adoff, A. (1973). <u>Black is brown is tan.</u> New York, NY: HarperCollins. ISBN 0-06443269-9.

Benton-Benai, E. <u>The Mishomis book: The voice of the Ojibway.</u> Red School House, Inc., 643 Virginia Street, St. Paul, MN 55103.

Cameron, A. (1988). <u>The most beautiful place in the world.</u> New York, NY: Knopf. ISBN 0-394-89463-4.

Carter, P. (1990). <u>Harriet Tubman and Black history month.</u> Columbus, OH: Silver. ISBN 0-671-69109-0.

Codye, C. (1990). <u>Luis W. Alvarez.</u> Madison, NJ: Raintree Steck-Vaughn. Spanish & English ISBN 0-8172-3376-8.

Codye, C. (1990). <u>Queen Isabella the first.</u> Madison, NJ: Raintree Steck-Vaughn. Spanish & English ISBN 0-8172-3380-6.

Coerr, E. (1977). <u>Sadako and the thousand paper cranes.</u> New York, NY: Putnam. ISBN 0-440-47465-5.

Crews, D. (1991). <u>Bigmama's.</u> New York, NY: Greenwillow. ISBN 0-688-09951-3.

Delacre, L. (1989). <u>Arroz con leche: Popular songs and rhymes from Latin America.</u> New York: Scholastic. ISBN 0-590-41887-4.

De Varona, F. (1990). <u>Bernardo de Galvez.</u> Milwaukee, WI: Raintree. ISBN 0-8172-3379-2.

Emberley, R. (1993). <u>My house, mi casa.</u> New York, NY: Little, Brown. ISBN 0-316-23448-6.

E-Yen-Shure (Blue Corn) (1939). <u>I am a Pueblo girl.</u> New York, NY: William Morrow. Out of print.

Garcia, M. (1987). <u>The adventures of Connie and Diego/ las aventuras de Connie y Diego.</u> San Francisco, CA: Children's Book Press. ISBN 0-89239-028-X.

Garza, C. L. (1990). <u>Family pictures/ cuadros de familia.</u> Emeryville, CA: Children's Book Press. Spanish & English ISBN 0-89239-050-6.

Gleiter, J. (1990). <u>Benito, Juarez.</u> Madison, NJ: Raintree Steck-Vaughn. Spanish & English ISBN 0-8172-3381-4.

Gobel, P. (1987). <u>Buffalo woman.</u> New York, NY: Macmillan. ISBN 0-689-71109-3.

Hewitt, J. (1990). <u>Hector lives in the United States now: The story of a Mexican-American child.</u> New York: HarperCollins. ISBN 0-397-32278-X.

Hoffman, M. (1991). <u>Amazing grace.</u> New York, NY: Dial. ISBN 0-8037-1040-2.

Hoyt-Goldsmith, D. (1992). Hoang Anh: A Vietnamese boy. New York, NY: Holiday. ISBN 0-8234-0948-1.

Isadora, R. (1991). At the crossroads. New York, NY: Greenwillow. ISBN 0-688-05271-1.

Johnson, A. (1989). Tell me a story mama. New York, NY: Orchard. ISBN 0-531-08394-2.

Jordon, J. (1994). Kimako's story. Boston: Houghton Mifflin. ISBN 0-395-60338-2.

Keller, H. (1994). Grandfather's dream. New York, NY: Greenwillow. ISBN 0-688-12340-6.

Kraus, J. (1992). Tall boy's journey. Minneapolis, MN: Carolrhoda. ISBN 0-87614-746-5.

Kusugal, M. & Munsch, R. (1988). A promise is a promise. Buffalo, NY: Firefly. ISBN 1-550370-09-X.

Langstaff, J. M. (1987). What a morning! The Christmas story in Black spirituals. New York, NY: Macmillan. ISBN 0-689-50422-5.

Levine, E. (1989). I hate English. New York, NY: Scholastic. ISBN 0-590-42305-3.

Lloyd, H. & Trimble, S. (1988). Our voices, our land. Northland. ISBN 0-87358-412-0.

Lowery, L. (1987). Martin Luther King day. Minneapolis, MN: Carolrhoda. ISBN 0-87614-299-4.

MacLachlan, P. (1971). Through Grandma's eyes. New York, NY: HarperCollins. ISBN 0-06-022560-2.

Maher, R. (1977). Alice Yazzie's year. New York, NY: Coward-McCann. Out of print.

Maruki, T. (1982). Hiroshima no pika (The flash of Hiroshima). New York, NY: Lothrop, Lee & Shepard. ISBN 0-688-01297-3.

Moran, T. (1988). An Inca farmer. Vero Beach, FL: Rourke Enterprises. ISBN 0-86592-144-X.

Musgrove, M. (1976). Ashanti to Zulu: African traditions. New York, NY: Dial. ISBN 0-8037-0358-9.

New Mexico People & Energy Collective (1981). Red ribbons for Emma. Berkeley, CA: New Seed. ISBN 0-89239-041-7.

Ortiz, S. J. (1988). The People shall continue. Emeryville, CA: Children's Book Press. ISBN 0-89239-041-7.

Stanek, M. (1989). I speak English for my mom. Niles, IL: Albert Whitman. ISBN 0-8075-3659-8.

Sumption, C. & Thompson, K. (1990). Carlos Finlay. Madison, NJ: Raintree Steck-Vaughn. ISBN 0-8172-3378-4.

Thompson, K. (1990). Pedro Menendez de Aviles. Madison, NJ: Raintree Steck-Vaughn. Spanish & English ISBN 0-8172-3383.

Thompson, K. (1990). Sor Juana Ines de la Cruz. Milwaukee, WI: Raintree. ISBN 0-8172-3383-0.

Tohona O'odham Tribal Council (1984). Tohona O'odham: Lives of desert people. Tohono O'odham Education Department, Post Office Box 837, Sells, AZ 85634.

Uchida, Y. (1993). The bracelet. New York, NY: Putnam. ISBN 0-399-22503-X.